Non-sexist Education for Young Children

A Practical Guide

96962

Barbara Sprung, *Educational Director*

> Non-sexist Child Development
> Project for The Women's
> Action Alliance

Citation Press   New York   1975

LIBRARY OF CONGRESS CATALOGING IN PUBLICATION DATA

Sprung, Barbara.
   Non-sexist education for young children.

Bibliography: p.
1. Educational games. 2. Sex discrimination in education. I.
Women's Action Alliance. II. Title.
LB1029.G3S67   372.1'3   75-22490
ISBN 0-590-09605-2

Photographs by Ann-Marie Mott

PUBLISHED BY CITATION PRESS, A DIVISION OF SCHOLASTIC MAGAZINES, INC.
EDITORIAL OFFICE: 50 WEST 44TH STREET, NEW YORK, NEW YORK 10036.
PRINTED IN THE U.S.A.
LIBRARY OF CONGRESS CATALOG CARD NUMBER: 75-22490

Cover design by Honi Werner

2 3 4 5   79 78 77 76

This guide is dedicated to the four centers where this project was field tested. They are: The Educational Alliance Day Care Center, Ann Gray Kaback, Director; Lexington Houses Children's Center, Shirley Cowan, Director; Mabel Barrett Fitzgerald Day Care Center, JoAnn Hoit, Director; and Amalgamated Workman's Circle Co-op Nursery, Catherine Hoviss, Director. Teachers, administrators, aides, parents, support staff, and, above all, the children breathed life into theories. Without their help, this guide to non-sexist education could not have been written.

A WORD ABOUT THE WOMEN'S ACTION ALLIANCE
370 Lexington Avenue
New York, New York 10017

The Alliance is a non-profit, educational organization, which was established in 1971 to help translate a growing awareness of sex discrimination into concrete actions and improvements in the lives of women. The Alliance offers information, research resources, model projects, a referral system, and other tools through which women of all economic and ethnic groups can work for both personal and institutional change.

The first model project undertaken by the Alliance was the Non-sexist Child Development Project; this Guide is the result of that endeavor.

Contents

Acknowledgments

The work of the Non-sexist Child Development Project was made possible through grants from the Eastman (Lucius and Eva) Fund Inc., the Chase Manhattan Bank, the Arca Foundation, the New York Community Trust, and the Ford Foundation. We thank them for their generous support.

The Ford Foundation grant was administered by the Department for New York City Affairs of The New School for Social Research, and we wish to thank Dean Henry Cohen and Associate Dean Jerome Liblit for their encouragement and backing.

The Project was carried out in 1973–74 by a staff of three: Carol Shapiro, Administrative Director; Jane Galvin-Lewis, Community Relations Director; and Barbara Sprung, Educational Director. In addition to the Project staff, all the other members of the Women's Action Alliance gave generously of their energy, time and skills; we thank them all for their contributions.

A special word of appreciation to Letty Cottin Pogrebin for sharing with us her expertise in the area of non-sexist child rearing and to Harriet K. Cuffaro who has advised us in the area of child development since the inception of the Project.

1 Background of the Non-sexist Child Development Project

In 1972, at the very beginning of its existence, the Women's Action Alliance began receiving mail from women all over the country who were concerned that their children were being forced into rigidly stereotyped roles, even in pre-school. The Alliance did some research into the problem and came to the conclusion that although people were working to reduce stereotyping at every other strata of education, virtually nothing was being done at the pre-school level. The Alliance felt strongly that non-sexist education should start at the beginning of a child's educational life rather than somewhere further up the line when much that had already been learned in a sexist way would have to be "relearned."

The Women's Action Alliance decided to undertake the development of a non-sexist early childhood program. It would free girls and boys of sex-role stereotyping and allow them to develop to their fullest potential, unhampered by societally imposed restrictions regarding appropriate behavior for each sex. The goals of the program are:

☐ To present men and women in a nurturing role so that children understand parenting as a shared responsibility.

☐ To show women and men performing a wide variety of jobs so that children understand that people are free to choose their work from an enormous variety of options unhampered by sex typing. In many cases, we have presented men and women in counterpart jobs to underscore the fact that most jobs can be performed equally well by men and women.

1

☐ To encourage girls as well as boys to engage in active play and to encourage boys as well as girls to enjoy quiet play. In all media, girls are overwhelmingly presented as passive creatures watching boys at play, while boys are presented as always active, unflaggingly energetic dynamos.

☐ To help boys and girls respect each other so that they can be friends throughout childhood and into adulthood. We do not mean that children of opposite sexes will always play together. Girls will want to be with girls and boys with boys much of the time. However, we feel that our social mores encourage this separation of the sexes rather than minimize it. We also feel that the way girls are presented in children's materials as passive, fearful creatures who strive constantly for adult approval helps to create the derisive attitudes boys have toward girls.

☐ To encourage boys and girls to develop and be able to express a full range of emotions. It is mostly boys who are shortchanged in this area. Very small boys are told, "Boys don't cry." They are expected to hold back when they are hurt physically or emotionally because to display feelings is considered a "feminine" trait and to develop any "feminine" trait is highly undesirable and leads to being called a "sissy." We want all children, and consequently all adults, to feel free to experience a full range of human emotions.

☐ To encourage the full physical development of all children. In this area, it is usually girls who are not encouraged at school or at home to develop their fullest potential. Boys and girls alike should know the joys of physical activity and be as strong and as fully developed physically as they are able.

☐ To present a more realistic (and therefore exciting) view of the world to children. We live in a pluralistic society made up of many varied racial and ethnic groups. Yet the world presented to children by the media and early childhood materials is overwhelmingly white. Although in recent years blacks have been more fairly represented, one hardly sees Hispanic, Asian-Americans, native Americans, or Chicano people in early childhood materials or early elementary textbooks.

☐ To present a more open view of the family. There are many alternative family groupings to the nuclear family. These alternative families can consist of two people or many people who live together and share food and shelter. A family can have one, many, or no children and still be a family. Although many of the alternative families are successfully and happily sharing life together, children are consistently presented the nuclear family as the norm and made to feel that their family is less acceptable if it does not conform. We would like to see teachers and children explore the variety of family life styles that actually exist side by side with the nuclear family and learn to accept and respect each of these family groupings.

At the onset of the project, we spent several months observing in twenty-five child care centers in the New York metropolitan area. We looked at the books on the shelves, the records and games, and the ways teachers and children interrelated. We arranged times for interviews with the directors of each center so that we could discuss our project and find out what the prime concerns of each center were. In each center visited, the idea of developing and using non-sexist materials seemed to cause the most excitement.

During the observation period, two centers volunteered to become demonstration centers. A third center was recommended because the director is a feminist. The fourth demonstration center, a co-operative nursery school, volunteered to join the project because parents had expressed an interest in looking into ways that they could free their children from the kind of sex-role stereotyping they had been subjected to as children.

Before beginning our work in the four centers in the fall of 1973, we spent many months exploring the possibilities of convincing manufacturers that there was a need and a market for non-sexist toys. It soon became apparent that it would be a long, slow process to have materials made commercially, so we did what teachers have always done when they need special materials—we made them ourselves. We handmade a set of prototype materials and used our first grant money to have six sets of them hand-produced.* This gave us a complete set for each of the four centers, plus two extra sets for the workshops we have given throughout the country over the years. In addition to our puzzles, lotto, flannel board, and block accessories, we put a library of non-sexist books, a set of resource photos, and a copy of the record *Free to Be You and Me* in each center. We also placed a tape recorder in each classroom so teachers would be able to record conversations and discussions with a minimum of fuss.

To create a program that would foster the goals set forth earlier, we decided to work with *all* the adults affecting the children's lives—teachers, administrators, aides, parents, and support staff members of each center. We felt that if our project was to have a lasting effect on the lives of children and was to bring about more than superficial change, our approach to non-sexist education would have to be a total one, including consciousness-raising with parents and staff members, non-sexist curriculum ideas, and new materials for the children.

Before introducing the materials in the classrooms, we met at least three times with teachers and other staff members in in-service sessions during which sexist materials and attitudes as well as the goals of the project were examined. In some centers we met with parents from the start, and in others we waited until the teachers were working smoothly with the program before scheduling a parent meeting. We found parents cooperative and enthusiastic. This is not to imply that parents were always in complete agreement with us. We had some very lively discus-

---

* A complete description of these materials, plus instructions for making those not yet commercially available, appears in the chapter "Non-sexist Materials."

sions about allowing boys to play with dolls. However, we found that parents were very willing to examine our points of view about non-sexist education. Although many of them felt that their own lives would probably not change much, they *all* wanted more open options for their children. In some centers the teachers were surprised at how accepting of the project the parents were. As one stated after a particularly stimulating and successful parent meeting on the topic of toys, "Well, we certainly underestimated our parents."

After we had conducted several consciousness-raising sessions with teachers, we presented our non-sexist materials and suggested ways of introducing them to children. Teachers were cautioned to present the materials slowly so that the children would have time to explore and question each one thoroughly. We urged teachers to treat our program as they would any other, that is, to slowly integrate it into the classroom life at a pace that was comfortable for the children. We wanted to stimulate the children, but overstimulation would have caused tension for them. We stated over and over that we would rather delay the testing than have the project interfere with normal classroom life. In one center we waited several months to begin because the children were adjusting to a new teacher, and we wanted them to be perfectly comfortable before the program was introduced.

The field testing took place from September 1973 until April 1974. During this time, in addition to regularly scheduled staff and parent meetings, we were available to the four centers as often as they felt they needed us. We made it clear that after the testing period was over, we would continue to be in contact and to help in any way we could.

Before moving to the non-sexist early childhood program itself, we feel it is essential to discuss briefly some facts of child development and the learning styles of young children so that readers will understand the framework within which we approached our task.

2 Framework of Child Development

This program for early childhood is rooted in what is known about the development of young children and their learning styles.

We would like to make explicit the philosophical stance that has determined our view. Obviously, it is free from the limitations of sex stereotyping and stresses being oneself rather than playing a role. As a corollary and intrinsic to our approach is the emphasis on supporting and fostering children's abilities to think evaluatively and discriminatively. In addition to an intellectual style characterized by the ability to be logical, inventive, and rational, we believe the total picture of children must include the feelings and imagination of the individual. We see in the interweaving of and the relationships between the cognitive and affective domains the integration that leads to a view of the whole child. Further, we see the individual in a social context, as a member of a community. Consequently, we emphasize social development, consider the school as a community of people—parents, children, teachers—and focus on learnings about jobs people do, their skills, talents, responsibilities, and their interrelationships.

We consider the assignment of traits to a specific sex as detrimental to the development of people. Why should boys and men be held back from being nurturing, gentle, expressive of feelings? Why should girls and women be

This essay is excerpted from an article "Psychological Theory and Child Development Background" written by Harriet K. Cuffaro, Bank Street College of Education, New York City.

denied a more dynamic personality? Our world is very different from the societies that started to train their young for the roles they would inevitably play as adults. If anything, the best preparation for the unknown future of today's children is that each be a whole person, utilizing as much individual potential as possible. If the current mode of alternative life styles is stabilized, then the environment will be more conducive to more options for both sexes. Our society does not need more definitive men and women but rather caring, responsible, capable, and imaginative *people*.

In the years of early childhood young children are engaged in the tasks of understanding themselves and others, the order of life, and unraveling of the mysteries of the adult world. Invariably children are seeking to understand their role in the world, "Where, how, and when do I fit into this reality?"

The tasks children undertake are rather formidable, especially when the "limitations" of their thinking style are considered. I say "limitations" only because the adult standard is orderly, logical thought, and children of three to six years are a long way from that criterion.

A young child deals with the world in a highly personalized, individualized manner. Fantasy and reality are manipulated and altered according to personal needs and desire. Children's viewpoints are very egocentric and narrow in perspective, and their functioning is further restricted by their tending to believe what they see. They have not mastered important skills yet. For example, it is extremely difficult for young children to attend to more than a limited amount of information at the same time. Because their focus tends to concentrate on one aspect of a situation, they miss relationships and they concentrate either on an undifferentiated whole or on parts or details. It is also difficult for young children to handle transformations as their attention focuses on the fixed state without incorporating elements of change into a process. To further complicate the situation, it is also difficult for them to go back in thought to the starting point and reconstruct the process of an action.

To illustrate some of these points, consider the familiar

juice time situation when one child decides to break up a cracker into small pieces and then announces triumphantly, "I have more than you do" to a child who has an intact cracker. Many crackers have been reduced to infinitesimal, uneatable crumbs as children try to have "more" crackers. It is fascinating to watch this situation consistently repeated and to observe the *time* children need to understand that one does not really have more crackers but only an increased number of cracker pieces. Reconstructing the cracker, putting the pieces together, and saying, "See, it's just like yours—*one* cracker!" is usually greeted by, "She has more," for the child is focusing on what is seen—more pieces—and not on the process by which the pieces were obtained.

Even with these "limitations" children three to six are developing an ever-increasing facility with language and the ability to function within the symbolic realm. The preschool child, unlike the toddler or infant, no longer needs a thing to be present for it to exist. For example, having known a dog by playing with it, touching it, or hearing it, a child can now imagine a dog, pretend to be one, recognize it by sound, and talk about it—all without an actual dog being present. This is abundantly evident in the dramatic play in the block area, outdoor play, and the house corner as children recreate the experiences they have had, the information they have absorbed, and the thoughts and feelings these evoke as they relive their experiences in their play.

The social development of children gradually becomes more and more expansive. They move from solitary play to associative play to cooperative play. With increased independence and autonomy, they progress from playing alone or in fleeting moments with others, toward playing alongside another or others with increasing continuity and in a more sustained, interested manner. With the development of increased social skills and emotional maturity, children begin to be able to plan with others, to amend ideas, and to engage in the give and take essential to cooperation within a group.

It is in the social realm that a child's egocentric viewpoint begins to be altered. As a youngster interacts with others, there are differences in opinion and viewpoint that affect her or his perspective. Children and the world interact as they explore it and come directly into contact with its institutions, opportunities, and roles. As they move further out into the world from self and family to school, to neighborhood, and to the world at large, they learn to create order by generalizing, classifying, sorting, enlarging, altering, reconstructing knowledge and understanding. Ordering includes not only information but also the realm of feelings, and play is an important means by which children learn.

Young children learn best through direct experience, participation, and interaction with the concrete, real world. They need opportunities for exploration and experimentation and time to question and to test ideas. As children learn about their world and themselves, our aim is to offer them, through our program, opportunities to find a more accurate reality, one unhindered by the burden of stereotypic thinking. As children classify and generalize about people and roles and as they learn about themselves, we want this to occur within a framework that focuses on human potential rather than prescribed societal limitations.

The learning opportunities offered in this book include direct experiences relevant to the immediate interests of young children and available within pre-school and kindergarten settings. Through discussions, materials, trips, games, books, language activites, and dramatic play, children have many opportunities to question, to try out ideas and to test them, and through their play to experience their understanding.

3 Involving Parents

It is as crucial for parents as for teachers to become aware of sexism in language and television. Language and television permeate every aspect of a child's life at home. Because of this, it would be ineffective if we tried to create programs in these two areas without involving parents.

SEXIST LANGUAGE

Sexist language is the most pervasive aspect of sexism in our society. We feel that masculine words, which are used constantly to convey broad human concepts and groups, contribute substantially to the "non-person" status so many girls and women feel about themselves.

Young children certainly *do not* understand that words such as mankind, brotherhood, early man, manpower, or chairman are supposed to include women and men in their scope. Even older children and some adults have a problem recognizing that these words encompass both sexes. These generic words contribute to the notion that women have not participated in the development of civilization.

Add to this the fact that the masculine pronoun, he, is used on all institutional forms (even if the group filling them out is 99 percent female), and it can easily be understood why so many females consider themselves second-class persons. Also contributing to the low self-esteem of women is the fact that they are encouraged to remain children throughout their lives.

When a culture makes adulthood synonymous with manhood, a girl can never reach adulthood at all. There is a clear demarcation between the words boy and man that does not exist between girl and woman. A boy greatly increases his stature when he becomes a man, but a girl loses status and bargaining power when she loses youth.[1]

Women are regularly referred to (and refer to themselves) as girls. Any man would consider it derogatory to be referred to as a boy if he is above the age of adolescence, but women of all ages are girls. (The term boy came under scrutiny in the civil rights movement as derogatory when used to refer to a mature black man.) When women are not called girls, they are often referred to as "ladies." Lady is a term that has an entirely different meaning than woman. It suggests helplessness and has class and behavioral connotations that woman does not. If the word lady is paired with gentleman, at least they both carry the same connotation, but when men and ladies are paired, as they most often are, the combination implies that women are unequal to men.

Other pairs of words that have very different meanings are master and mistress and bachelor and spinster. In each of these the masculine word is positive and complimentary, while the feminine counterpart connotes being owned (being a mistress) or being rejected (no one chooses spinsterhood).

In a study done by American Heritage Publishing Company prior to the development of its wordbook for children,[2] some startling facts about sexism in language were discovered. A computer analysis of five million words encountered by American school children in their books was carried out. It was found that when adults write for other adults, they often use the words child or children, but when they write for children, they carefully differentiate and use the word boy or girl twice as often. Also, no matter what the subject matter of a book, girls and women are in a minority even though they comprise over 51 percent of the population. The overall ratio of masculine

---

1. Graham, Alma. "The Making of a Non-Sexist Dictionary," *Ms. Magazine*, Dec. 1973, pp. 12–16.
2. *American Heritage School Dictionary*. Boston: Houghton Mifflin, 1972.

pronouns to feminine is four to one. Men and boys are the subject matter of most of the stories. The study found over *seven* times as many men as women in the books and over *twice* as many boys as girls. However, when one sees how girls and women are portrayed in these books and becomes aware of the words associated with females, one may be glad that they don't appear more often!

In a study titled "Sexist Semantics in the Dictionary" by H. Lee Gershuny,[3] an analysis was made of the sexism in the *Random House Dictionary*. It was found that masculine gender words appeared in 68 percent of the sample and feminine gender words in 23 percent with the mean 9 percent masculine or feminine. Female gender words were found to connote weakness, dependency, incompetence, vanity, submissiveness, timidity, and the like. A few female positives were sensitivity, nurturance, and tenderness. Masculine words connoted achievement, ambition, aggression, competitiveness, competence, dominance, and intelligence.

In other words, the patterns of viewing males and females with both a sexist and stereotyped point of view exist in the dictionary and in the vast body of books that help to shape children's views of society.

It is no wonder that boys show derision to girls! One cannot help feel negatively toward people who are constantly described as afraid, incompetent, foolish, gossipy, or stupid, and this is the way not only girls but women are overwhelmingly described (when they are described at all) in printed matter. Such views of themselves and their adult role models are destructive to the self-image of girls. We also consider the constantly active, competitive, non-emotional, non-nurturant view of males that is presented in books to be damaging to the self-image of boys. They cannot but feel pressured or inadequate trying to emulate the role models of the adult males presented to them through books.

What can teachers and parents do to change sexist lan-

3. *A Review of General Semantics,* vol. XXXI, no. 2, June 1974, pp. 159–68.

guage and to free children from these damaging images? First, as always, we can become aware of the language patterns, which we may be using unconsciously, that perpetuate sexist views. For example, it is considered grammatically correct to refer to both sexes as "he," but is correct grammatical structure worth a lessened self-image for even one female child?

We can begin to consciously refer to children as children or people and avoid saying boys and girls so much of the time. We can refer to humans, humanity, people, brotherhood, and sisterhood instead of man, mankind, and brotherhood to express the concept of global civilization. We can use words that connote strength, intelligence, humor, tenderness, nurturance, achievement, when we discuss *both* men and women and girls and boys. We can, when absolutely necessary, use the more awkward forms s/he and his/her, rather than leave half the population out of our speech. As we read books aloud to younger children, we can edit them to make them less sexist. We will have to do this for a while until some new books are available. No one is suggesting that the vast body of children's literature be eliminated because it is sexist. We can change wording whenever possible and make children aware of some of those changes. With slightly older children, it is a good consciousness-raising technique to let *them* find the sexist messages in their books.

Another thing we can do is to become aware of how often we comment to little girls about their looks. Are we assuming that we add to their self-image when we compliment them on their appearance instead of their accomplishments? Do we say, "Steve is strong" and "Eve is pretty?"

Finally, if we use non-sexist terms for workers in the community, children will soon begin to use them also. Children are imitative and often use the same phraseology as their teachers and parents. So, if we say letter carrier instead of mailman or mail lady, police officer instead of policeman or police lady, chairperson instead of chairman or chairwoman, delivery person, spokesperson, fire fighter, and sanitation worker, instead of dividing them by sex, children will learn these terms correctly from the beginning and will not have to go through a relearning process in elementary school.

In 1972, Scott, Foresman and Company issued the first set of guidelines for eliminating sexual stereotypes, *Improving the Image of Women in Textbooks* and in 1974, McGraw-Hill Book Company issued *Guidelines for Equal Treatment of the Sexes in McGraw-Hill Book Company Publications*. Most recently the School Department of Holt Rinehart & Winston has published *The Treatment of Sex-Roles* for its editorial staff. All these publications are available by writing to the issuing company. The McGraw-Hill guidelines are especially well thought out and give many helpful ideas about how to restructure language to avoid sexist attitudes and still maintain good grammatical form. It really is quite possible to do both.

TELEVISION

Many of us think of television as an overwhelming force in the lives of children over which adults have very little influence or control. Parents, in particular, feel this way. Although they may thoroughly disapprove of what their children watch, they feel powerless to prevent them from watching.

We have tried to give parents the feeling that not only can they control what their children watch, if they are determined to do so, but that they can also help to turn even very young children into critics who are aware that the men and women they see on television are absurd and unrealistic people.

Teachers can do a great deal to help children and parents become more aware of the harmful images seen on TV. We suggest that teachers engage the help of parents for a "Critical Look at TV" discussion. If possible, have parents and other people who care for children come to a special meeting to discuss ways in which they can help children become more critical viewers. If a meeting is not possible (often working parents are too tired and busy to come to an extra meeting), speak to the persons who pick the children up at school and explain that they will be bringing home "homework" about TV. It is also possible to inform parents with a letter, although personal contact is preferable.

We think the poem "I Hate Housework," from the record *Free to Be You and Me* (see Bibliography), is a good way to start a discussion of how silly women and men often act on TV. Another way to start a discussion is to say, "I saw the silliest commercial on TV last night." The children will almost surely follow with silly stories of their own.

Assign the children some watching for one night and have them report about what they saw the next day. Try to have the children compare the men and women they have seen on commercials with the adults with whom they interact daily. Do their mothers, grandmothers, aunts, or baby-sitters discuss soap and floor wax all day? Do the men in their families lead an outdoor life or exclaim over glossy floors and dirty rugs the way men on TV do? Ask parents or guardians to sit and watch TV with their children for a short time each evening; let them know the assignment so they can become involved in the children's viewing and help point out some of the absurdities. We feel that enlisting the aid of someone in a child's home with the assignment will not only help the child, but also the person watching with the child, to become more aware of the images of men and women the children are bombarded with daily.

Helping children become critical of television can do more than combat sexism—it can also help them become wiser consumers. Again, by enlisting the help of parents, teachers can make children aware of the poor quality and lack of durability of many of the toys advertised on TV. The most effective way to do a comparative study with children is to have them bring in a collection of their toys, including TV toys, and compare them with the toys in the classroom for durability and interest. Have parents help by showing children when they go shopping together the toys that break easily and are "junky."

Taking a look at food commercials, which regularly advertise sugared cereals, candy, and other tooth-rotting foods on children's shows, is a natural follow-up activity for The Human Body unit described later. As children learn about their bodies, they will certainly need to know the effect food has on health and growth.

After studying TV in the ways suggested above, teachers can suggest that the children compose a letter to a major network (or several) to protest their advertising and programming. Younger children can dictate what they want to say, and older children can write their own letters to a network or to particular advertisers. Parents and community people can also start letter writing campaigns to protest not only sexist commercials and shoddy merchandise but excessively violent programming as well. These campaigns can be quite effective. Advertisers are only too aware that a displeased audience means a loss of sales.

TV plays a large role in children's lives and will continue to do so. Therefore, it seems of prime importance that we begin to deal with it educationally and do all we can to make it a positive rather than a negative force.

PARENT-STAFF MEETINGS

As stated in the opening chapter, it was basic to the philosophy of our project to involve all of the key adults in the children's lives in our work. Before beginning, we decided that we would only work in centers where there was a nucleus of people, parents and teachers, who wanted nonsexist education for their children. We felt that if we went into centers where the goals of the parents and teachers were very different from ours, we would set up a situation of conflict for the children. This would be counter-productive both for them and for the project. This premise proved to be a sound one. In each center, our relationship with parents evolved differently, but working with each group was a valuable experience in which parents were as helpful to us as we were to them. We will now share the techniques that we found most valuable in our contact with parents.

The way to begin is similar to the way we begin exploring any area of thought—find out what people think and feel about a given subject. One way to start is to schedule one or more informal meetings on the topic of educational goals, physical and emotional development, working mothers, the meaning of play, or any similar subject that the center staff and administrators feel would generate a good discussion. It may take some time until a relationship is established between staff and parents that allows for free and open discussion, but it is better to invest the necessary time before embarking on educational changes for which the parents may be unprepared. In the Mabel Barrett Fitzgerald Day Care Center the Director, JoAnn Hoit, had alread spent a good deal of time establishing such a relationship with parents before we began to work in the center. They had advanced from casual discussions about equal pay for equal work and the need for day care as the parents brought the children to school in the morning and picked them up in the evening to full-scale meetings on such topics as sex-role stereotypes. In the words of Ms. Hoit:

But something did change when we talked about the children. Our first official discussion was called sex-role stereotypes. About twenty-five parents and staff attended: black, Hispanic, white—mostly women and a few male staff and parents. Together we wondered why we used boy/girl groupings so often to move the children through routines, "Now all the *boys* put on your coats and go to the yard." We wondered why art was a girls' activity and boys weren't supposed to play with dolls in the housekeeping area. People shared their hopes that their children would marry and have children and explored their fears about homosexuality. We talked about what it means to find an identity: racial, sexual, human. We talked about the right of every individual to find an answer on his/her own terms. We talked about helping our children to grow up free by helping them to try out as many of their talents, interests, and roles as they want to.

It is clear from the above quote that the parents in this center were far along in their thinking and discussions of topics pertaining to the women's movement. They were ready to evaluate sexist materials and look at non-sexist alternatives for their children. In two other centers, the topic of sex-role stereotyping had never been specifically discussed, and our staff and the staff of each center did quite a bit of thinking and planning for the initial parent meeting. The staff of the Educational Alliance, Anne Gray Kaback, Director, was sensitive to and aware of the particular social mores of their parent group and suggested that we not use the words sex role or sexism in our discussion. Based on their insights, we planned a meeting around the topic of toys. The timing was excellent because it was scheduled just prior to the holiday toy-buying season. The turnout was very good because we had chosen a timely and important subject.

We emphasized throughout the meeting that we did not want any child deprived of the learning inherent in any toy. Each teacher and each of our three staff members took turns explaining the learning possibilities of our favorite toy or type of toy, and each of us stressed that the toy was equally important for girls and boys. We also stressed the quality, safety, and longevity of each toy; we urged parents to begin helping their children to become quality-conscious consumers. After our presentation we opened the meeting for discussion and had an exchange of views that lasted nearly an hour. One mother told all of us that she had insistently given her daughter a doll every Christmas, although the girl showed little interest in doll play and preferred trucks. She told us that this Christmas she would give her child *both* a doll and a truck!

The toy meeting was so successful that we shared the idea with another center. The staff of the Lexington Houses Children's Center heartily agreed that the toy approach would be a good way to reach their parent group also. The format of the meeting was a bit different. The Director, Shirley Cowan, went to some of the leading distributors of early childhood materials in the New York City area and purchased a selection of sturdy, safe, educational toys, books, and records. In addition, we supplied copies of several nonsexist books and the record *Free to Be You and Me*. The parents were able to browse and select their holiday toys right at school before the meeting, which took place in the early evening over sandwiches and coffee.

Again, after we presented our views about toys and explained why we felt it was important to let boys and girls learn all they could from all types of toys, we opened the meeting for general discussion. Parents were eager to participate and share their feelings about toys. We had a fruitful discussion about toy guns—whether they were useful because they provided children with an outlet for aggression or harmful because they encouraged violent play. People spoke up on both sides of the issue. Ms. Cowan explained the school's philosophy that no toy guns were allowed, but the children were permitted to use imaginary symbols (such as a pointed finger or a block) if their need for a gun was strong enough to make them invent one. This compromise seemed to satisfy most people, although some still said they saw no harm in toy guns and would continue to let their children play with them.

One parent shared this story with the group. She told us how much she had wanted trains when she was a little girl and could not have them because they were for boys. She, of course, said that she was planning to buy her daughter a set of trains for Christmas.

Another interesting incident occurred at this meeting. The director had inadvertently picked up two paperback picture books that were sexist when she was purchasing the materials. They served as a dramatic example of how carefully we must examine everything bought for children if we want to avoid adding sexist materials to our homes and classrooms. In each case, Ms. Cowan had picked the books because she knew other works by the author, but she had not examined each page of the text, It was the kind of mistake all teachers and parents make, and she graciously gave me the two books to add to my collection of sexist early childhood materials.

In our fourth demonstration center, the Amalgamated Workmen's Circle Co-op Nursery School in the Bronx, Catherine Hoviss, Director, our work began differently. In this center the parents had initiated interest in looking into sexism. At our first meeting we looked at sexist puzzles and books and then viewed and discussed *Dick and Jane as Victims* (see page 101), a slide show depicting sexism in elementary school readers. The mothers in this center were most articulate in stating the conflicts that their perception of the women's movement caused in them.[4] Most were women who did not work outside the home, and many of them had chosen homemaking as a full-time profession, at least while their children were small. They felt something should be done to help women such as themselves to feel less guilty and more positive about having made the choice to stay at home. The concern expressed by these mothers led us to create the unit on homemaking described later.

Although our work with parents began differently in various situations, we had the same goals, not only for the parents in the four demonstration centers, but also for the thousands of parents we have reached in the workshops we have conducted nationally. These goals are:

☐ To help parents become aware of sexism in our society.

☐ To help parents become aware that sexist attitudes affect the way we handle children from birth on.

☐ To help parents become aware that sexist attitudes and behavior deprive children, both girls and boys, of the opportunity to develop to their fullest potential.

☐ To help parents become aware of everyday influences, such as language, television advertising, and packaging, and how these perpetuate sexism in ourselves and our children.

☐ To help parents become aware of what they can do to combat sexism in general and in the lives of their children in particular.

☐ To mobilize parents to conduct letter writing cam-

---

4. The phrase "perception of the women's movement" is used because we view this as a misunderstanding of the women's movement rather than a fact. The women's movement has consistently tried to present homemaking as *one* option open to women and has tried to upgrade the self-image of women who work in the home.

paigns against sexist advertising, packaging, and programming on television.

☐ To mobilize parents to raise the issue of sexism in their local public schools.

AREAS OF GREATEST CONCERN

Before we began working with parents we tried to anticipate the areas that parents would be most anxious about. We defined these as homosexuality, doll play, and biological sex differences. We then researched these subjects so when questions arose, we were prepared to defend our view that no aspect of our philosophy would increase homosexuality, confuse children's proper sex-role identification, or interfere with biological sex differences.

When the question of homosexuality arose, one project director always made the point that although we live in a society rigidly divided along sex lines, homosexuality is rife and perhaps we should be open to looking at new ways to rear children. We also referred parents to several studies on sex-role identification, one of which is Mussen and Distler's *Child Rearing Antecedents of Masculine Identification in Kindergarten Boys* (see Bibliography). This study clearly makes the point that, contrary to popular belief, the most positive sex-role identification takes place when the sex roles between parents are *less* rigidly defined and when the father is warm and nurturant rather than a stern, authoritarian stereotype of the father figure. We found that being able to refer to studies on the subject alleviated parental anxiety and gave credibility to what we were saying.

Concerning doll play, *William's Doll* by Charlotte Zolotow (see Annotated Bibliography of Children's Books) turned out to be as useful a book to read to parents as to children. Its approach to the question of why a little boy might want or need a doll is a common sense one. Parents usually ended up nodding their heads in agreement when the grandmother, who gives William a doll, explains to William's father why his son needs a doll:

"He needs it," she said,
"to hug
and to cradle
and to take to the park
so that
when he's a father,
like you,
he'll know how to
take care of his baby
and feed him
and love him
and bring him
the things he wants,
like a doll,
so that he can
practice being
a father."

Most parents and teachers have never stopped to consider that boys have as much right and need to examine the role of fatherhood through doll play as girls have to examine the role of motherhood.

When this writer brought *William's Doll* home for her family to review, her son confessed that he had played with his sister's dolls as a little boy but *only* behind closed doors. He then polled his friends, and each of them who had a sister, and therefore access to dolls, said he had done the same thing! I regularly relate this anecdote to parents because it conveys an important message—all of us have been conditioned to think and act in certain ways, and it takes a conscious effort to begin to think more openly. But we can change and if we do, we will help children to become freer than we were. It helps parents to know that other parents have made mistakes, even those they might consider experts.

We also made the point that although we deny little boys the opportunity to try out the role of fatherhood through doll play and other nurturant experiences and systematically teach them to inhibit their emotions, we somehow expect them to grow to adulthood and miraculously become tender, affectionate, sensitive partners and fathers. Again, whenever we made this point to parents, their heads would nod in agreement.

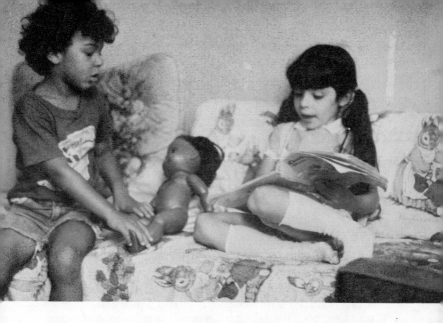

To prepare ourselves for questions concerning biological sex differences, we did much reading on the topic. We also attended a lecture given by Susan Ralls, a biologist who was then teaching at Sarah Lawrence College in Bronxville, New York. Ms. Ralls' lecture clarified for us any questions we might have had about hormonal differences, pre-natal development, and the difference, if any, in the male and female brain. She unequivocally stated that there was no difference between a female and male brain. This made us feel entirely comfortable with our philosophy—to offer as many options as possible to boys and girls and let them make their choices from these options as human beings, not as males and females. In discussions with parents and teachers, we tried to emphasize that we would like to see new research undertaken and older research reexamined in the light of new information that has become available since the 1960s, when the latest phase of the women's movement got underway.

Parents were as helpful to us as we were to them. Their insights into their own children and social groups were enormously important to the way we shaped the programs in each center. They shared their work with the children and helped us to find interesting trips for the children to take. If it hadn't been for one alert husband, we might not have been able to give the children the experience of seeing a woman building engineer (see *Jobs People Do*).

In another center, a father's reaction to the slide show, *Dick and Jane as Victims,* was to go into the public school to investigate what books were being used to teach his children to read. In the same center, parents and teachers arranged a meeting with community people and the local kindergarten teachers to share all the non-sexist materials with them. Since this center is a cooperative, it has a volunteer program called Mother of the Day. It is now called Parent of the Day, and at least one father is giving a full morning of his time to the center each week.

We have shown parents both sexist and non-sexist materials and have explained why we feel non-sexist materials are superior. Through discussions, we tried to make them aware of the dangers of sexism to both boys and girls and to spur them to take action to combat it whenever and wherever they can. We made the basic assumption that no parent wants less than the fullest intellectual, emotional, and physical development for her or his child. All our work with parents was geared to helping them become aware that for children to realize their fullest human potential, sexism must be eradicated from their lives.

4 Creating Non-sexist Environments

When the Women's Action Alliance began to think about developing a non-sexist early childhood education program, we sought advice from experts in the field. Their comments usually ran something like this: "Why us? We have been letting boys and girls do the same activities for years. Why, we even allow coed toileting!"

This is perfectly true. Most pre-school programs do not openly segregate activities according to sex. Girls may not be encouraged to use the woodworking bench nor boys the housekeeping area, but they are seldom overtly denied an activity if they choose it for themselves. Also, it is true that most pre-schools in the United States do not have separate toilets for boys and girls; this provides at least one opportunity for children to gain some knowledge about their bodies and the biological differences between male and female.

This situation does not exist, however, in most kindergartens, where very often toileting is separate and where boys seldom, if ever, feel free to choose the playhouse as an activity and girls seldom, if ever, build with blocks. By first and second grade the divisions are almost complete; a youngster who even shows a desire to engage in an activity specified for the opposite sex knows that he or she is in for peer ridicule as well as adult disapproval.

Separating people according to sex roles is traditional in Western civilization. Each of us, consciously or unconsciously, helps to perpetuate this division by transmitting cultural attitudes that we may have accepted without careful examination. People who work with young children have a unique opportunity to challenge and change cul-

25

tural stereotyping. They are the ones who provide children with their initial experiences outside the home. They not only become the most important influences on children outside of their families, but they have the added advantage of working with and influencing children's families more than at any other phase of their education. They also rely less on printed materials in their work with children and are freer to innovate and create experiences for and with them.

Although teachers are concerned with cognitive skills and physical development, the primary goal of early childhood education is the positive social and emotional development of children. To help children develop healthy self-images, we must foster and nurture the whole child and allow him or her to reach his or her fullest potential, unencumbered by rigid sex-role stereotyping that is equally damaging to the growth and development of both female and male children.

Those of us teaching in early childhood classrooms have a *responsibility* to look into ourselves, our attitudes, our classrooms, our materials, and our work with parents to recognize the many subtle ways in which we perpetuate sex-role stereotyping. We must begin to devise methods in all areas to eliminate these stereotypes from the lives of children.

THE HIDDEN MESSAGES

A group of feminist teachers in California participated in a study conducted by Carole Joffee (see Bibliography) to examine the hidden messages teachers give to children. A trained observer spent time in each room and watched the teachers at work. They made some startling discoveries. They noticed that, despite their feminist philosophies, the teachers tended to pay more attention to girls when they came to school wearing dresses! They profusely remarked about how pretty they looked, reinforcing once again the societal message that it is how a girl (and later a woman) *looks* that is of primary importance.

As teachers and parents become more aware of the ways they transmit sexist messages, they begin to notice many things about their language, their classrooms, and their materials, such as toys, books, and records. Suddenly a line or phrase in a book they have been reading for years will stand out as sexist. *Dear Garbageman* by Gene Zion (Harper & Row, 1957) provides an example. A teacher had been reading this book to children for years when one day she noted this sentence, "After everyone had helped themselves, Fathers went to work and Mothers went back to the dishes." The teacher described her reactions to this seemingly innocuous sentence as follows:

I guess I had read that book to children countless times over the years without realizing what a message that one line was giving on several levels. First of all, many of my children had working mothers, and here was one more line in a book that left their mothers out. If you add up all the times working mothers are left out of books and other materials for young children, it is no wonder that children often think that something is wrong with their family when mother works. Also, it struck me that to describe the mother who stays home by saying, "Mothers went back to the dishes" is a very demeaning description of homemaking. Picking the most menial of chores to represent what mothers do can't help but add to the low opinion children and adults in our society have of the job of homemaking.

Maybe it seems picayune to dwell on one line in one book, but sexist attitudes are made up of a conglomeration of just such sentences. They may be in a book, on a record, in a TV commercial, or in a situation comedy. They are in the pictures of men and women that decorate classroom walls. They are in the illustrations of lotto games, puzzles, flannel board figures, and charts.

Take a look at the materials in your classroom. Are all the community worker block accessories male except for the nurse? Is it possible to use the female block accessory from the family group as anything but a homemaker? Do any of your materials depict males in a nurturing role or females in work roles other than homemaker? Are there any books about children living in one-parent homes or in families other than nuclear families?

Teachers help perpetuate stereotyped views when they

fill their dress-up areas with absurdly feminine hats, shoes, and pocketbooks. These frilly props equate femininity with uncomfortable, dysfunctional clothing that perpetuates pseudo-beauty as *the* female goal. The dress-up apparel in most classrooms is reminiscent of the kinds of ridiculous outfits the goose and hen (usually foolish creatures such as Petunia) wear in children's books.

Even more important than the multitude of external messages mentioned above are the attitudinal ones teachers and parents pass along unconsciously. A teacher described how she became aware of and changed the way she discussed clothes with children:

I used to remark about the children's clothing frequently. I did this to help them to become observant of themselves and each other, to develop color sense, and to generally enhance their self-images. I used to be careful to say that girls were pretty and boys were handsome. When I became aware of sexism, I began to examine what I was saying to the children. Instead of pretty and handsome I used words that connoted comfort and function. "Short sleeves are cool and comfortable for today, David." "Those overalls are great for climbing, Nell." or "I like the color combination you chose today, Peter."

Just by changing the ways I looked at the children's clothes, I was influencing their attitudes toward appearance without diminishing their pleasure in color or denying them a special bit of attention. As a matter of fact, it made giving each child a real bit of attention easier since my comments become subtler and less hackneyed than the clichés pretty and handsome.

This teacher made a simple change in just one aspect of appearance—clothing—but just as sexism comes across to children through a variety of messages, non-sexist attitudes can be passed along in similar fashion.

Changing sexist lines and phrases in books as we read them (no one is suggesting that teachers throw out books that have some sexism in them), hanging pictures in classrooms that do not perpetuate sexist stereotypes, modifying the props given children for dramatic play, and becoming aware of their own language patterns and changing them whenever possible are but a few simple things teachers can do to begin to alleviate sexism in their classrooms. And these small things do make a significant difference! A teacher recently described the following incident:

I really notice a freer attitude in my room this year, probably because I'm more aware myself now. Recently I put up a picture of Roosevelt Grier doing needlepoint in my housekeeping corner. You know the one—it's an ad for Interwoven Socks. Well, a few days after I put it up one of my little four-year-old boys brought *his* needlepoint to school! You know that none of this would have been possible a few years ago.

HOUSEKEEPING AREA

Although some early childhood educators minimize it and Montessori schools eliminate it altogether, the housekeeping area, sometimes known as the dress-up area, playhouse, doll house or Wendy house, is a staple of most early childhood classrooms. In this segment of the room most of the dramatic play about family life takes place. It thus provides teachers with many opportunities to observe the sexist attitudes of children as they reflect their own family lives. The important first step in creating a non-sexist program is always to find out what the children's perceptions and understanding of a given situation are and then devise experiences that will offer more options and a more open point of view. Here are some ways teachers can open up the housekeeping area and begin to free it of its ingrained role divisions.

Clothing and props What kinds of male and female clothing does it have? Does the female clothing consist of frilly hats, pocketbooks, lots of beads and earrings, spike-heeled shoes, and long, fancy dresses? Does the male clothing consist of fire hats, construction helmets, man-sized jackets, and shoes? If so, these props are helping to perpetuate stereotyped views of men and women. By simply changing the selection to more comfortable contemporary clothing, changes can begin to be effected.

For example, one teacher noted that by providing more small suitcases and briefcases and fewer pocketbooks more boys and girls began playing dramatic roles about going to work. Most men's clothing is so large and unmanageable for little boys that they tend to dress up less than girls. Instead of using adult male clothing, try larger boys' sizes in jackets, shirts, and shoes. These are much more comfortable and encourage use. Tailored shirts make comfortable, functional dress-up clothes for both girls and boys; for instance, a work shirt is a good construction outfit for boys and girls. Half slips make fine skirts, which fit far better than women's dresses, and simple short nightgowns with shoulder straps make "fancy" dresses that are easy for children to handle. It is also a good idea to have some lengths of material and cloth that the children can fashion into any costumes their imaginations dictate.

Dolls Educators and parents are aware of the important role of dolls in the dramatic play of children. A doll is one of the first abstract symbols used by children to replace the self as an object of play. We want and expect girls to explore the nurturing role and mothering through the use of dolls, but this medium is almost totally denied to boys, although logically they have just as much need and right to explore the nurturing role and fathering. It is ironic and sad that we condition our little boys away from doll play and then are angry and resentful when as adults they seem unable to show affection, tenderness, and nurturant qualities as husbands and fathers.

There are several things teachers and parents can do to make doll play more acceptable and attractive to boys. The first is to examine our own attitudes. Are we uneasy that encouraging doll play for boys will disrupt their formation of proper sexual identity? Are we afraid of parental or community objections? Are we ready to accept doll play as an important developmental experience for boys as well as girls?

The importance of a nurturant father in the development of proper sex identification with same-sex parents is discussed by Mussen and Distler (see Bibliography) who found that the *more* nurturant the father is and the less rigidly defined the roles of the parents, the more likely a positive identification with the parent of the same sex will occur. Behavior that conforms with male stereotypes such as authoritarian, stern, or distant is much more likely to cause fear in children and result in a negative identification with the parent of the same sex.

If teachers are to encourage doll play among boys, they should have more boy dolls in their classrooms. It is unfortunate that most dolls are anatomically incomplete, that is, they have no sex organs. This undoubtedly gives children the impression that their sex organs are something to be secretive about. It is certainly a source of confusion to them, since other parts of dolls' bodies are usually quite detailed, e.g., baby dolls have dimples, folds, and navels.

We understand that anatomically accurate male and female dolls are available in stores in many European countries, notably in Sweden. To date, it has been a losing battle in the United States to obtain anatomically complete, reasonably priced dolls. The one company that had advertised them in its catalog recently withdrew them because of lack of sales.

However, we can at least give boys and girls dolls that are as physically like themselves as possible. Classrooms should contain girl and boy baby dolls and girl and boy dolls that look like young children three to six years old. Such dolls do exist, and they will help encourage doll play, especially among boys. When we put a black male doll dressed like a typical five-year-old in our demonstration centers, there were dramatic results.

In one center, a little boy who had seen the black boy doll Caleb [1] the afternoon before, came in the next morning and asked, "Where's *my* boy?" In another center a teacher related this story to us:

The day after you brought the Sasha doll to us, I introduced him to the children at our circle time. I received "oohs and ahhs" and much excitement. The children identified with him, giving him names such as Samson, David, Bruce Lee, and other names of strong, powerful men. They said he was five years old and loved his friends. The biggest and most pleasant surprise came when K. demanded David (the name we all agreed

1. Creative Playthings, Princeton, N.J., 08540. This doll is part of the Sasha line.

on) from me and hugged him closely with all his strength. He refused to share the doll and kept holding him close to his body with enormous strength. Eventually I talked him into sharing the "feel" of David with the rest of the group who had grown quite impatient and angry. K. wanted to monitor the passing around of David, so I agreed. He did not allow any child to hold David for more than a few seconds.

I was flabbergasted by this behavior. Never had I seen such caring and tenderness expressed by K., who had grown up with the conception that life is tough and one had to be tough to survive. He could not play with dolls and rejected such tender, "sissy" enjoyments. And now, here was K., holding on to a doll!

All that day K. kept David with him. He ate, slept, and played with the doll. The following day he washed David's clothes, and when they were dry, he ironed them.

For an entire week K. played with David and included him in every phase of classroom life. Later on in the week, the doll corner became of interest to K. and, not only David, but most of the other dolls became a part of his experience. David not only brought a new happiness to K. but afforded him an outlet through which he was able to express kindness, tenderness, and love. He no longer stood in the background watching others express fondness and warmth.

Pictures, Books, and Staff If teachers believe that homemaking and parenting are shared responsibilities of men and women, they should have pictures in the housekeeping corner that show both sexes caring for children and performing household chores. Such pictures will help boys feel freer to try homemaking and nurturing roles and will also serve as catalysts for discussions about their own families and how work is divided in their homes. Books can also fulfill this function. A teacher told us about her experience reading Charlotte Zolotow's *William's Doll* (see Annotated Bibliography) to three-year-olds:

The first time I read it I got no reaction at all from the children. We had no discussion following the story that day. The next time I read it we had a marvelous discussion about all the things their fathers did for them. I found out how nurturant many of their fathers were in bathing, feeding, and dressing them. These were not things the children discussed spontaneously as they did about the nurturant things their mothers did.

Even at three they perceived their fathers and mothers stereotypically, despite the reality in their own homes, which contradicted the stereotypes.

I find the conclusion of the story particularly moving (see page 22). It sparked the children to talk about the nurturant role their fathers filled in their lives. With this knowledge, I was able to create other opportunities for them to express this aspect of their fathers' behavior, and it soon became a natural topic of discussion for us.

If a child care center or kindergarten is fortunate enough to have a male staff member in the classroom, he can become an enormous asset by frequently making himself available to the children in the housekeeping area. He can be a living example of a nurturant male, and if he and the female staff share housekeeping chores of the classroom together, they will provide the children with attitudes and experiences that convey far better than words that the processes of daily living are naturally shared by women and men.

COOKING

Closely related to the housekeeping corner, yet serving a more strictly functional purpose, is cooking. Cooking enhances an early childhood program on many levels. It is a life skill that requires knowledge of math, science, safety, language, hygiene, nutrition, and aesthetics. When children cook, all their senses, as well as their intellects, are involved in the process. It would be hard to find another life skill that calls for such a fusion of abilities and feelings. With all its inherent possibilities, it seems a real educational disservice to deprive a child of either sex of the cooking experience. Yet cooking is often conceived of by parents and teachers as appropriate only for girls. Children invariably perceive of cooks as women, despite the fact that many men cook for a living, and chefs with the most status and prestige are usually male.

The stereotype of the woman cook abounds. Few fathers share this job at home, and on TV, cooking is one of the few things women are shown doing. In children's books, mommies are always baking or preparing dinner or lunch. Daddy is shown eating but never preparing food. Whitney Darrow's book, *I'm Glad I'm a Boy—I'm Glad I'm a Girl* (Simon & Schuster, 1970) has a page that reads, "Boys can eat. Girls can cook." The implication is that boys can't cook and girls can't eat.

To counterbalance this very prevalent stereotype and stop denying boys the pleasures and learning that cooking brings, teachers and parents must do everything they can to see that both sexes feel free to cook in school. How can this be done? It bears repeating that young children learn best through example and experience.

If children see men cooking, it will help them accept cooking as a skill performed by *people*. If male staff is not available to cook with the children, arrange for a male family member to come and do it. If this is not possible (usually all you have to do is ask), there must be some male member of the community who would be delighted to share his skill with the children. Try to vary the ages of the visiting cooks. Perhaps a grandfather, uncle, or teen-age boy would help out as well as a father-aged per-

son. This will help reinforce the feeling that cooking is a life skill all people need to have.

Pictures and Stories As in the housekeeping area, pictures of boys and girls and men and women cooking will greatly help children to feel this is an acceptable and desirable activity. Pictures can help children express negative feelings as well as positive ones, and they offer teachers opportunities for one-to-one discussions with children. Sometimes a discussion may arise spontaneously, and sometimes the teacher may ask a question to start it. Stories also serve this function. If you cannot find stories about men and boys who cook, make them up, have the children make them up, or use a stereotypic one about women and girls cooking to start a discussion about whether it is accurate to show only females cooking.

Even very young children know the importance of food and, because of this, cooking can have a very prominent place in the program. Young children are always very interested in any skill that will make them independent, and cooking is something all independent people need to be able to do for themselves.

Finally, American adults have notoriously poor eating habits, which make them fat and less healthy than they should be. Through cooking experiences good nutritional values can be instilled in both boys and girls. By teaching children to cook food that is tasty and good for them, by using ingredients that are natural, by conveying enjoyment and patience, and by avoiding the use of mixes and artificial ingredients, we can help children understand that to feed their bodies well and to be healthy are important functions of life.

BLOCKS [2]

Block play is one of the major activities of any early childhood classroom for a very good reason. Working with

---

2. This section on blocks is based on a longer piece on the same subject by Harriet K. Cuffaro, Bank Street College of Education, New York City.

blocks contributes to the physical, social, cognitive, and emotional development of children. To put it more succinctly, blocks complement the development of the *whole* child. Also, blocks are not limited to a specific age level. They are used by children over a wide age range. They are unusually durable when made of wood, and they lend themselves to countless building and dramatic play activities. Children can construct houses, garages, schools, launching pads, bridges, and many other structures. It is possible to come back to a building one has begun and enlarge it, change it, or simply play with it again the next day. This constancy is reassuring to children who live in a rapidly moving and changing world.

Block play offers children a wealth of intellectual as well as social experiences. Both mathematical and physical laws are concretely demonstrated. Children learn about balance, force, support, and gravity as they build. Only through the experience of putting large blocks on top of smaller ones do they come to "know" that a structure will topple over if it is built this way. It takes much experimentation before they learn to build foundations with strong support at the bottom, and block building is an ideal medium for such experimenting. Concepts of mathematics and geometry are inherent in the unit blocks used in most early education settings. They are constructed with a geometric unity that is a pleasure for children to discover. For example, there are single, double, and quadruple unit rectangles in each set, and these can illustrate fractions and multiples, two triangular blocks form a square, and two semicircles form a circle. These are but a few of the mathematical concepts children handle daily when they are involved in block building. Through such play, mathematics becomes a useful, understandable tool for daily living and not an abstract principle to be learned by rote.

In addition to experiencing physical and mathematical concepts, children are engaging in a cooperative, decision-making activity when they work with blocks, and this makes it a socially important experience. Of course, children do not always build with others. Even if a child is making an individual structure, she or he is still sharing the floor space and equipment with other builders, and this is where both the art of compromise and knowledge of math is applied. On the average day in any school, children will find it necessary to use two double units if the quads are all used up, to negotiate with other builders for the gothic arch, or to share the block accessories. They must also carefully choose a floor space that is not too close to another builder or to the block cabinet, or else they run the risk of having their building destroyed! These experiences help them to understand themselves in relation to the space around them and to respect another person's spacial needs as well as their own—a most valuable concept in our crowded world!

Block play is an excellent follow-up activity for social studies trips into the community. Again indicating the concrete learning style of young children, they enjoy translating trips into block schemes when they return to the classroom. They may build a town, neighborhood, school block, or visit to the river; any trip they take is translatable into blocks. Working on block schemes provides children with a group experience that fosters cooperation and is usually highly pleasurable for them. They will develop dramatic play situations along with their buildings, taking the part of people they have seen on their trip.

Obviously, blocks are a material that support children's development in an integrated, organic way and offer almost limitless learning opportunities. It would be unreasonable to restrict their use to only some children and deprive any of the rich potential inherent in their use. Yet blocks are generally considered boys' material, thereby closing the door to a wealth of opportunities for countless girls. Why does this happen? Building with blocks is associated with architecture, construction, engineering, and "making things work." It requires participation that is active, physical, and accompanied by noise and much "figuring out." In short, in the cultural terms of traditional Western society, block building characteristically falls into being a man's world. In classroom after classroom, blocks are the boys' domain. When children are directed toward play, the invitation, "Do you want to work in the block area?" is not often extended to girls. It does not take a girl very long to read the message. No encouragement or invitation from the teacher, the absence of girls building, and the activity and bustle of the area, which run counter to what a girl has been taught is appropriate "girl behavior," all result in girls considering this area as unavailable to them.

It might be of interest to consider what can happen when emphasis is placed on the learning opportunities offered by a material rather than on the gender of the child. At the City and Country School in New York City, which was founded by Caroline Pratt who designed unit blocks, block building is the core of the educational program for ages three through seven. It is, of course, seen as appropriate for all children. Within such an atmosphere, it is not surprising that girls in this school build daily and find it as interesting and satisfying a material as do the boys. Girls build complex buildings, interesting architecturally and in terms of content. In this school the invitation to participate is explicitly extended to all children—as are cooking, woodworking, sewing, and physical activity—without regard to traditional sex lines. Given the opportunity, girls demonstrate an ability to use blocks and find them satisfying and challenging.

In the four centers where this project was tested, we discussed the importance of block building for *all* children during our in-service sessions with teachers. Within weeks we noticed increased participation in this activity on the part of girls, and just as we suspected, not only did the frequency of their building increase, their structures grew larger and more ambitious!

Based on the evidence of schools such as City and Country and on our own experiences in the four test centers, it would seem once again as if awareness on the part of teachers is the key to opening up new learnings for children. If teachers are aware of the potential of blocks for both cognitive and affective development and if they share their understanding with parents, they will help both girls and boys to extract the fullest possible learning from this material.

Here are some specific suggestions to stimulate block play:

☐ When children are ready to start the day, as suggestions are made and questions asked, make block building one of the activities consistently mentioned to girls, as it is usually offered to boys. Go one step further by saying, "You know, I haven't noticed you using blocks, that might be a fine place for you to work today." To extend this even further, a couple of girls might be approached with, "What would you like to build together?" or "Remember when we went to the store to buy fruit yesterday? Maybe you can make a fruit store with the blocks. I'll come and help you get started." Of course, teachers' statements will depend on the age level, the individual child, and the life of the classroom.

☐ Once girls do start building, both boys and girls must be helped to accept the situation. Girls might need consistent encouragement for continuity of effort. Boys might need help to accept an "intrusion" into male territory. This might be particularly true in situations where girls seldom enter the block area and when boys are active, engrossed participants.

☐ Discussions, especially with kindergarten age children, are a definite asset in promoting and extending the dramatic play that accompanies block building. In group discussions teachers can be mindful of including girls through questions, comments, posing of problems, and drawing them into the group situation.

☐ Trips are necessary for sustaining and extending block play. This is the constant source for replenishing and refueling the content of dramatic play, since the focal point of such play is the reconstruction and reformulation of reality. Trips to local stores, fire stations, and the like are known standbys, but in these very familiar resources one will find sexist pitfalls. Girls must be able to find exciting, challenging roles to emulate from experiences in the real world. Such roles will be easier to locate as sex barriers in the job market fall, and girls will find women in a variety of interesting positions. Meanwhile, teachers must make special efforts to locate women who are plumbers, carpenters, police officers, construction engineers, marine biologists and other jobs that excite and stimulate the imagination of children.

☐ Many accessory materials such as rubber and wooden people, supplement block play. Until recent years, these have been stereotypic, standardized figures. Not only have the professions represented among community workers always been male (with the exception of a lone nurse), but for many years there were further limitations in that the father was pictured with a newspaper and the mother with apron and a baby painted in her arms, thereby making it impossible to use the female figure for anything other than a mother role. We are pleased that there are now available on the commercial market multiracial male and female community workers to be used with blocks. This will certainly encourage girls to participate. As one eight-year-old girl said upon seeing these new figures, "Oh, this will make pretending much easier."

Other accessories added to the block area should be examined for possible sexist connotations when selecting materials. Choose things that are useful to *people* when they *work*.

It has often been suggested that one way to encourage the participation of girls in the block area is to declare a "girls' day" or set up times when only girls can build. We strongly advise against this practice. It might lead to block *building* for a day but not to the creation of block *builders*. Segregation even for seeming noble ends cannot work because it is inherently unfair and places girls in a false, untenable position. It may take longer to get girls into being functioning, fully participating group members in this area of the classroom, but the additional work and time will produce the results we really want for children who are to be free to be themselves.

OUTDOOR PLAY

Outdoor play offers enormous potential for children to move fully through space, an impossibility in the classroom, regardless of its size. It is mainly outdoors that large motor development takes place through such activities as walking, running, climbing, wheeling large objects, and swinging. Muscular development also occurs by carrying hollow blocks, large boards, saw horses, and similar materials that are simply too large to fit indoors in most schools. Ball games, running games, and other activities that increase coordination are also best suited to outdoor play.

This is not to say that all outdoor play must be vigorous and involve running and shouting. Dramatic play occurs outdoors as often as indoors. However, although house play certainly occurs outdoors as well as indoors, outdoor dramatic play is more likely to involve transportation (driving a bus or train, riding on a boat), hiding, chasing, and escaping (robbers, Batman), building large structures (spaceships and stations, airplanes), and generally requires louder voices and larger, freer movements. Even sand and water play take on different dimensions under the sky. Outdoors children needn't be much concerned with the consequences of spilling and splashing.

Finally, there is the sense of joy and freedom that the larger outdoor space provides; children express this, not often in words, but in running, shouting, and jumping as soon as they move from indoors to out.

Unfortunately, not all of the above-mentioned joys are experienced by many girls, for it is outdoors where one sees the clearest division of children along sexist lines. By the time they reach pre-school, too many female children have already learned that it is considered unseemly for girls to use their physical selves with abandon. It is expected that boys will be noisy, dirty, and physical and that this is normal and contributes to their growth and development. Girls are not expected to get as dirty as boys, and they are taught that they must be careful of their clothes and appearance even at three years of age! These expectations stifle freedom of movement, and it can safely be said that by the early elementary years many girls have developed an aversion to physical education and outdoor play, which is directly related to the societal messages they have been receiving.

What can teachers and parents do to free girls (and some boys) of the inhibitions that keep their outdoor play from being the source of learning and physical development that it should be? First, as in all other areas, they must heighten their own awareness of the messages they give children. A teacher who was examining her own attitudes about outdoor time told us:

I realized that I was the perfect role model of the shivering, inactive female for my class. I feel the cold very easily, and I found myself standing in a state of frozen tension, so constricted that I could hardly move, and counting every moment to "going in" time. Then I decided to do something to improve my situation and the image I was presenting to the children at the same time. I began to wear warmer pants and to bring lined boots on cold days, and I kept an extra old sweater near the cubbies. But, more important than dressing, I learned some exercises that increase circulation. One of these is used by police officers on the beat and consists of vigorously swinging your arms across your chest! Naturally, the children were fascinated by this aspect of a police officer, and many little cold ones began to imitate my exercise, thereby warming themselves instead of begging to go inside. I also ran in a large circle and soon the Pied Piper syndrome would take over and I'd have a following.

When I thought about it, I had done nothing inventive, just two or three common sense ordinary things, but they helped me and my children cope with cold weather so much more effectively!

Another thing teachers can do is to refresh their own thinking and then articulate the goals of outdoor play to parents. Very often parents are unaware that outdoor play has an important rationale in the pre-school program and consider it as just a fun time for the children with no educational purpose. Usually, there is a meeting with parents at the beginning of the school year, and this is a good time to acquaint them with the educational importance of the outdoor time.

Also, teachers have to ask themselves if they are bothered, due to their own conditioning about what is appropriate behavior, by girls who are loud and play as roughly as boys. If they think that it is not appropriate behavior for girls, the girls will pick up this feeling with that special instinct children have for adult disapproval. Conversely, if the expectation is that all children play vigorously, the children will also pick this up.

Recently, we were observing outdoor time in one of our demonstration centers and were immediately struck by the different quality of the girls' activities. They were vigorous, not house play oriented; they ran, climbed, shouted, and were thoroughly adventuresome. When we discussed our observations with their teacher, she told us it hadn't always been that way. She said she had made herself a role model, often running and playing ball and always encouraging this kind of play. Our visit was in February, and her attitude and encouragement had already produced the changes we had seen. Incidentally, she was the same teacher who had been so successful in freeing boys for doll play as described on pages 31–32.

Another way to encourage children is to take every opportunity to make them aware that climbing, jumping, and running help them to grow. Children are always fascinated when they become aware of a process, and they will surely better appreciate and understand their bodies if their insights into how they grow are increased. This knowledge is part of the healthy self-image we want all children to have.

Circle games, pitching games, and ball games are some of the more structured activities that may help involve less active children. Often children make up variations of the popular games.

Although all of the above suggestions are ones that will help children toward a more active use of the outdoors, we do not want to imply that this is the only kind of play we feel is important, nor do we want to lose sight of the fact that timid boys will need as much help to achieve full use of the outdoors as girls. It is important to remember that during outdoor time, as in all other areas of an early childhood program, the goal is to have both girls and boys participate as fully as possible. To strike a balance, teachers may need to encourage the more passive boys and girls and guide the most active ones to an appreciation of quieter activities. Naturally, some children will strike their own balance and need little or no guidance.

CLOTHING

It may seem irrelevant to discuss clothing, but clothes affect how children participate in every area of early education work, especially outdoor activity.

All children should come to school in "work clothes," for play is children's work, and they need to be comfortable and free to work in whatever they wear. This idea of wearing suitable work clothes to school is a part of pre-school tradition and was pioneered in such New York City schools as City and Country, Bank Street Children's School, Ethical Culture, and Little Red Schoolhouse in the early 1920s. In these schools children's play was treated with a serious attitude and with respect, for it was understood that through play children acquire the many skills they use in more formal education later. The educators who directed these schools realized that to be free to play, children must be dressed in work clothes and not the conventional school clothing considered appropriate in most schools at that time. In the words of Caroline Pratt, founder of City and Country School:

Of course the visitor was right in her complaint: this did not look or sound like any schoolroom. But it was very much like something else. It was like a segment of grown-up activity, an office, a small factory, or perhaps office and factory combined. Nor did these children look like school children, starched and clean-faced, the boys in white shirts, the girls in crisp frocks. These children wore work clothes, dungarees or overalls, *boys and girls alike* (occasionally a dress, the exercise of individual prerogative), and they and their work clothes bore the evidence of their work. [3]

To use blocks and to roll vehicles across the floor, children must wear coveralls so that their knees do not get hurt. Work clothes are essential for the child who paints, makes collages, cooks, or does carpentry. No one, grown-up or child, likes to do these sorts of activities in constricting clothes.

The other major factor about clothing that affects children's performances is that it be appropriate for the weather. If children are overdressed or underdressed, they will not be comfortable enough to move freely or feel relaxed for indoor or outdoor play. Although boys are sometimes dressed inappropriately, girls usually suffer the most discomfort in school because they wear dresses and fancy accessories, such as party shoes, which slip on most school floors and certainly are not conducive to climbing. It is also the nature of girls' clothing that causes them to feel cold more frequently than boys. Dresses are loose fitting garments that allow air to flow up. This is very cool in summer, but very cold in winter. Very often parents feel that tights take the place of long pants or overpants for girls, but since tights are not usually made of warm materials, this is not necessarily true. They do work well, however, as an insulating layer when they are topped by overalls or pants.

We do not mean to suggest that girls must never wear dresses to school. Many girls pass through a stage where wearing dresses is very important to them. Perhaps one reason they go through this stage is because they perceive that they receive much more adult attention when they look "pretty" as the Joffee study revealed (see Bibliography). In any case, if they are allowed to wear a dress or smock top, with pants underneath (for outdoor and indoor protection), they are usually satisfied, and this solution is certainly preferable to a morning confrontation that sets the tone for an unhappy day in school. Also, if

---

3. *I Learn from Children.* New York: Simon and Schuster, 1948.

children know that their teacher expects them to wear work clothes, sets an example by wearing them also, and has the support of their parents that this is what everyone wears to school, there should not be much of a problem.

If teachers explain to parents the rationale for the clothing preferred for school and make it clear that their children will be better able to fully participate in activities, we are sure they will cooperate.

WORKBENCH AND SHOP

Workbench or shop experiences provide young children with life skills that every independent person needs to know—how to construct useful items from wood and how to mend and fix. Shop also provides endless opportunities to use mathematics in an applied way and concretely demonstrates to children the importance of this skill. In addition, shop is one of the more product-oriented activities for young children and provides a sense of accomplishment in making something.

Very young children (three and up) are able to competently hammer, saw, and nail with much less adult help than most people think. Again, it's a question of expectations, and children will quickly feel an adult's sense of confidence or lack of it and perform accordingly. In addition to adults often underestimating *all* children's ability to work with tools and wood, shop is one of the areas in a classroom or school where sexist attitudes are most blatant.

Carpentry and construction has been a "man's" job through the ages. Whitney Darrow, in his now infamous (and out-of-print) book *I'm Glad I'm a Boy—I'm Glad I'm a Girl* states it all in six words: "Boys build houses. Girls keep houses." Indeed, schools in America have kept this idea alive by excluding girls from shop and boys from home economics courses until very recently. Many schools still have exclusive practices and probably will continue to until parents, students, and teachers pressure administrators to obey Title IX of the 1972 Education Act, which prohibits such discrimination. Our attitude is that to become independent adults who are capable of caring for themselves, boys and girls need to know at least basic carpentry *and* basic home economics skills. The time to begin teaching these skills is in the pre-school years.

Remember the math and science skills that can be learned in shop. One must measure, count, balance, and level to construct properly. Rhythm and coordination are involved in hammering and sawing. Judgment and estimating skills are also learned. One must be well-organized and plan ahead for the size of the nails needed, the thickness of the wood, the shape of the construction, and the trimmings it will need.

No child should be excluded from experiences that provide such possibilities for learning. Yet girls are usually systematically excluded from shop experiences because Western society has deemed this activity appropriate for boys only. Even in schools where boys and girls do woodworking, it has been observed that boys are given more independence and encouragement than girls. Many shop teachers seem to think that girls are less capable and require more help. Typical remarks heard go like this: "That's fine, Ted—you can do it all by yourself." "Here, Mary, let me help you with the nailing. We don't want any hurt fingers."

If teachers and parents want their children to have mutual respect for each other and if they agree that both girls and boys have equal needs to become competent, it is their job to help them acquire skills they will need to do so. To succeed, they must stop fostering less competent behavior in girls by perpetuating a double standard of expectations.

ARTS AND CRAFTS

Easel painting, making collages, drawing, clay work, sculpturing a variety of materials, sponge painting, finger painting, printing, stitchery, and a host of other art and craft activities provide children with opportunities to increase hand-eye coordination, small muscle control, attention span, and self-discipline. They also provide important training and increase readiness for reading and writing. But even more important than technical training, they provide children with a means of self-expression, a sense of aesthetics, and the pleasure that comes with creating.

Any person who has ever seen the joy of discovery and sense of beauty as three-year-old children experience the principles of color mixing through finger painting realizes the cognitive and affective importance of the art experience in early childhood. This exciting synthesis of sensory and intellectual learning that art provides should not be denied to any child, nor should it be limited in any way by different expectations of achievement for boys and girls. Since virtually no one consciously limits children's art experiences according to their sex, it may seem odd to even bring up the matter. But it is worthwhile to look at people's unconscious messages and the attitudes they convey in this area of art by asking ourselves some questions.

Do we have stereotypic views of what girls' art looks like? Is it more inclined to be pretty, with flowers and houses as a main subject? Do we think of it as neater than boys' work? Do we view boys' art as more complex? Do we expect their collages to show more glue? Are boys clumsier with their fingers? If these are our attitudes as we look at children's art, how do we convey them? If we consistently say to a girl, "That's a pretty picture," we may keep her creativity at a "pretty" level. If approval is associated with "pretty," the girl may feel she dare not try something that may turn out not so "pretty," but could be more complex and interesting and perhaps move her expression to a higher level of development.

A suggested way to move away from stereotyped comments to children is to discuss some aspect of the painting in more specific terms such as, "I like your color mixing. How did you make that bright orange?" or, "You have worked hard and have made many interesting designs today." These are comments that are pertinent to the work actually done by a child and less evaluative of aesthetic quality. If this type of statement is made to both sexes, children will understand that there are similar expectations for all. We noticed in our classroom observations that just as teachers suggest block building as a work activity more often to boys than to girls, they suggest painting and other art work less often to boys. A teacher told us:

As I became more aware of "hidden" messages I was giving children, I started to make a conscious effort to involve girls in block building and boys in art work more often. It was really so simple. If I saw a girl who did not seem to have a clear idea of what she wanted to do, I suggested blocks and sometimes offered to help her get started. I did the same thing with boys and art work. Just by lending a little support at the beginning of the work (I was always careful to move away as soon as I was no longer needed), I found the children were working in more areas of the room. Also, I saw girls' block building develop simply because they were acquiring more experience with the materials, and the same thing happened with boys and art. I used to think that girls were more dexterous than boys, but now I think that the reason they are is because they have more experience with cutting, pasting, drawing, etc., and the practice is what makes the difference. I want to continue to observe my children now that my expectations for them are not so stereotyped. I wouldn't be at all surprised if girls, who have as much encouragement as boys to build, and boys, who have as much encouragement as girls to do art work, turn out to be more equal in ability than I used to think.

This teacher expressed exactly what we anticipate happening to attitudes about young children. Our goal is to have teachers and parents view children as people who have strengths and weaknesses and likes and dislikes, because they are individuals and not because they are categorized according to gender.

5 Early Education Programs

When the Women's Action Alliance began to field test its non-sexist early childhood education program, each teacher in the participating demonstration centers was given an outline with suggestions for discussions, trips, and follow-up activities. We deliberately offered only suggestions because we wanted the teachers to feel free to create programs of their own. We encouraged them to use our ideas flexibly, realizing that what might work well for one group might not work at all for another. The overall goal was to create units of study out of the interactions between our suggestions and the teachers and between the teachers and the children. We wanted all the people involved in the centers, including administrators, parents, and kitchen and cleaning help to contribute their ideas—this is precisely what did happen during the months we worked in each of the four centers.

Inevitably there is some overlap in the following units of study especially in those of Families, Jobs People Do, and Homemaking, but this is true of all learning.

FAMILIES

Families are what young children know best. The first source of learning for young children is the family unit in which they live. Within the structure of the family, the child learns all the beginning life skills and emotions—to eat, crawl, walk, talk, to be loved, and to return love to those adults who give nurturance and care.

Who does a family consist of? If one looks at children's books and games, television, and advertising, it would appear that almost all families are white and consist of a mother, a father, and two children, usually one of each sex. This family group, the "nuclear family," is continually displayed as typical when in reality, in the United States today, there exist many different groupings that are also "families" in that they are two or more people who live together.

All who work with young children are aware that an increasing number of them live in a family that is not the nuclear stereotype. Twelve percent of all United States children live in one-parent homes headed by a female.[1] The number of children living in one-parent homes headed by males is as yet miniscule, but it is growing, and teachers should be aware of this trend and ready for the occasional child for whom this is a family reality. Another rare but growing trend is the interracial family, and teachers must be prepared to have materials and curriculum ready to serve a child from such a family. The block accessories designed by the Women's Action Alliance should be a helpful tool if such a child is a member of one's class (see Non-sexist Materials, chapter 6). Unfortunately, the extended family is not growing; however, many American children still do live in extended families. In certain parts of the country a new form of the extended family, the communal family, is a growing trend.

The point is that "family" is a concept that is currently fluid and changing. By constantly presenting children with a rigid and inflexible view of family, we may be confusing them. One of the main jobs of early childhood programs is to help young children understand the world around them. If the most important aspect of a young child's world, his or her family, is presented in a way that has no basis in his or her reality, we are doing an educational disservice to the child.

However, if children are presented an open view of family life with variety of groupings and life styles, no one will be left out of a study of families; all the children will feel free to include their family in the discus-

---

1. Roby, Pamela. *Child Care—Who Cares?* New York: Basic Books, 1973, p. 3.

sions. Teachers will also expose children to the fact that many kinds of families exist and that they accept and respect all of them.

How to Begin The best way to build any unit is to begin by finding out what the children already know. This enables teachers to avoid spending too much time on material that is already familiar and well understood. It also clarifies, at the outset, any misconceptions children may have about a given subject, in this case families.

One suggestion for starting a discussion about family is to read a story about one. Instead of choosing a typical story with the proverbial "nuclear" group, try one such as *Joshua's Day* by Sandra Surowiecki or *Martin's Father* by Margrit Eichler (see Annotated Bibliography), which are about children who live in one-parent homes. If the children you teach are predominantly from one ethnic or racial group, it would be better to choose a story dealing primarily with that particular group. However, if such a story is not readily available, the teacher can make one up or use a story about an animal family, which has no fixed ethnic or racial identity, to start the discussion.

After the story the teacher might say, "Let's talk about families today." Try to give all the children a turn to say something about their own families. If the group is too large to do this without inducing restlessness, try dividing the group in half and having two separate story and discussion times. At the end of the first discussion, sum up the information given by the children and stress the *variety* of facts they have given. Suggest that there is so much to learn about the families in the class that you should all talk about the subject on another day. You might want to give the children a question to take home to ask their families and report on for the next discussion.

At the beginning of the next discussion, it would be a good idea to summarize the previous one, asking the children to recall what they remembered so that you are certain no misconceptions are being formed. You might suggest that you will write down what the children say on an experience chart so that they can have a record of their study of families. Of course, as the children express what they already know, it is the job of the teacher to expand, clarify, and organize the material. For example, if a child mentions that an uncle lives in the family, the teacher can make sure all the children understand how an uncle is related to one parent, to the other parent (if there is one) as an in-law, to the child, and to the child's grandparents.

Visits After the children have talked a few times about their individual families and have written an experience chart so that all the information is recorded, it would be a good idea to schedule some school visits by members of the children's families. Personalizing of this sort is very important to young children. Try to invite the least stereotyped people first. For example, if an uncle or grandfather or teen-aged brother cares for a child, try to have this person come to school and share part of the morning with the children. We do not mean to imply that a mother or father is not welcome to visit, but these are the easier experiences to arrange, and since we want to open up the children's views on family, other less conventional visitors should be especially sought out.

Through these visits, it is hoped that the children will be exposed to men and women of all ages who spend part of their time caring for children. We feel this will help combat the stereotyped attitude that only women are nurturant and that only mothers take care of children's needs. Also, a unit such as this is an excellent way to involve family members in the school life of a child. People often feel they are not welcome in school, and this unit should help them to feel more needed and welcome.

Older people are isolated from children and vice versa, but they have much to share, and school is an excellent place for them to come into contact with each other. Also, older people have more free time than parent-aged adults who often work and are too tired to do much participating in school life.

One way to dramatize the visit of a family member is to have a special place in the room where, on the day a particular visitor is expected, the block accessory family figure who most closely resembles the visitor is displayed with a sign stating the visitor's name and relationship to his or her child.

Making Family Books Books made by the children are a fine way for them to record their family study. Each child can make an individual book to take home and also contribute to a class book on which all the children collaborate and which becomes a part of the class library. Each child can dictate to the teacher what she or he wants to say about his or her family for the individual book and then illustrate the story with drawings. The class book may be a round-robin story, to which each child makes a contribution, or a collection of individual stories that are bound together.

Another possibility is to let the children make up stories about family life. However, if the stories are fictional, it is important that the teacher help the children to understand the difference between an autobiographical and an imaginary account. Young children often confuse fantasy with reality. While we don't want to stifle imagination, it is important they be helped to distinguish between the two.

Puppets and Skits Often children who have difficulty expressing themselves can do so more easily through the use of puppets. Puppets can be made simply with paper bags and sticks, or the non-sexist family block accessories can easily be used as puppets by attaching pencils or sticks to the figures with rubber bands so the child will have something to hold. Children can enact simple family situations of their own devising, or the teacher can give a subject such as, "Let's pretend the mother puppet is going to work and the child is staying home with a sitter," and let the children act this out.

The possibilities for creating puppet skits that help children express emotions concerned with family living are endless. In these skits, children will reveal many anxieties that will give teachers greater understanding and enable them to be supportive and to design effective activities for each individual in the class.

Some children will be able to be themselves in dramatic skits and will not need or want to use puppets. Activities similar to those suggested for puppets can be planned. Again, either the children can choose simple scenes to act out or the teacher can assign short situations revolving around topics of family life.

Dramatic and puppet skits are excellent ways to help children express all the human emotions, especially the ones adults usually avoid dealing with such as sadness and fear.

Charts, Murals, and Other Art Activities During the early childhood years most of the skills needed for later success in learning are established. For this reason early childhood educators organize the day in a set routine, establish easy methods for setting up and cleaning up activities independently, set rules for story time that encourage quiet listening, ask questions that develop discussion techniques, and in many small ways foster the cooperative group behavior children need in order to learn.

It is possible to help even very young children learn to categorize and record their growing body of knowledge well before they have mastered numbers and letters. For example, when studying families, teachers can first record on a chart the members of each individual child's family, using the child's name and a stick figure for each person in the family. After the children are thoroughly familiar with this chart, the information on it can be consolidated into a chart that records by groups, such as mothers, fathers, grandmothers, grandfathers, aunts, uncles, and so on, the combined adults in the children's lives. This chart can be made with color bars, and the children will readily be able to tell if their families have more aunts than grandmothers, fewer uncles than fathers, or a host of other comparisons. Such simple charts are a form of symbolization that help prepare the way for the abstract thinking necessary in later school years. While abstract thinking is not the sphere of the young child, things that serve as experience building blocks leading to its full development certainly *are* a part of early childhood education.

Murals and collages are two more ways to tie family

study into other areas of curriculum. For family collages cut a variety of figures, or parts of figures, out of magazines (be sure to get a good racial mix) and have the children make a collage of a family. This should be a very open-ended activity where the children feel free to exercise imagination and whimsy. It should be both fun and interesting to see what they create.

A nice finale to a family study would be to have all the children—all those who want to, that is—participate in creating a family mural. A variety of media (paint, crayon, collage) could be employed, and the children can plan with their teacher the format they want for the mural. After the mural is completed, it would be a good idea to display it and the other art works, charts, and books related to the unit and give the children a chance to discuss their feelings about the family study in which they have participated.

Summary All early childhood programs contain some study of the family. Families are what the young child knows best, and there are many possibilities for expanding and enhancing this base of knowledge.

The main thrust of a family study is to help children broaden their views of family. We want children to both accept and enjoy the fact that there are many variations in how many people make a family and who these people are. It is a formidable task to fight the media stereotypes, but the schools are the best places to begin to do so, especially if they can enlist the cooperation of the children's families. Together, school and home comprise the largest force influencing a child's life. If teachers help children to feel as positive as possible about their own families and to accept and respect the families of their peers, they will also be helping them to build a positive self-image about themselves. However, to do this, teachers must first look more broadly at their concepts of family. They must learn to appreciate and respect the variety of existing life styles and must convey this appreciation and respect to their children through both attitudes and classroom projects.

JOBS PEOPLE DO

The world of work is fascinating to young children. Especially interesting to them are those jobs performed in their immediate neighborhood, the functions of which they can readily understand. The so-called community jobs such as fire fighter, police officer, letter carrier, construction worker, doctor, and nurse are those that are most comprehensible and seem most exciting to young children. Until very recently, however, all of these community jobs (except nursing) were performed exclusively by men. Studying the jobs performed in the community furthered the view that it is the men in our society who perform all the important jobs. Even the former terms for these jobs perpetuated the idea that they could only be performed by men, e.g., police*man*, fire*man*, and post*man*. This notion of male dominance is further perpetuated by the media and in early childhood books and materials.

For example, in the 150 readers examined by Women on Words and Images for their study and slide show *Dick and Jane as Victims* (see Bibliography), only two stories about mothers who work outside the home were found. In one, a woman works in the cafeteria in the same school her daughter attends, and in the other story the implication is that the boy, Martin, is a sullen bully because his mother is at work instead of at home! Also, until very recently, block accessories consisted of a community workers set containing eight figures, seven males in a wide variety of roles and one female nurse. In the only two family groups previously available, the black mother has a striped, ruffled apron painted on her, and the white mother has a baby painted in her arms.

Such materials certainly restrict children's views of the work women do. It must be very difficult for a child of a mother who works outside the home to understand why women are always portrayed in domestic scenes. It is also impossible to use a female figure dressed in an apron or holding a baby in any imaginative play other than house play. Readers and other materials similarly restrict the view of men's roles. Men are always portrayed as active, energetic, positive characters who never despair, never share household chores, or never nurture their children. Furthermore, the materials now available and the programs they inspire do not even adequately reflect the realities of present society, never mind presenting a forward-looking view. There are at least 26,000,000 American school children who do have mothers who work outside the home. Yet, despite this huge and growing figure, the working woman is virtually non-existent in the world shown to young children.

In perpetuating the myth, consciously or unconsciously, that homemaking is the only role women may play (we consider full-time homemaking as one of *many* options), teachers and parents are doing a double disservice to children. First, they give a false impression and confuse those who have working mothers, and secondly, they perpetuate the inequality of women by presenting so few options for them to choose in adult life. In effect, they tell boys and girls that, while boys may choose to be fathers and have any career they desire, girls may *only* choose motherhood. However, it is possible, within the framework of a traditional early childhood program, to open up children's views of the world of work and present it to them as much more equally shared by men and women. It is well worth the extra effort to present this more realistic view of work to children; to do so makes children more accepting of people performing non-stereotyped jobs and also shows the many choices they can consider for their own careers in adult life.

How to Begin As in the other units, we feel it is best to begin by finding out what children already know. What is their understanding of work? Who performs what jobs? If you ask children a controversial question such as, "Can a man be a nurse," don't be surprised if you receive a completely sexist response even from three year olds!

To begin a discussion about work, teachers might read a regular stereotyped book about jobs and then follow it up the next day with a more contemporary book such as Joe Kaufman's *Busy People and How They Do Their Work,*

Joe Lasker's *Mothers Can Do Anything,* or Eve Merriam's *Mommies at Work.* (see Annotated Bibliography). The differences between the first and second story should be a catalyst for raising some important questions about work.

Another way to begin is to show the children some photographs of women and men who are engaged in non-stereotyped work and have them react to them. One of the teachers in a participating demonstration center began looking at jobs in just this way. When the children were choosing work for the day, she offered them the option of making a book with some photos she had. Three girls chose this work and the following ensued:

On the table were 8 x 10 inch black and white photos of women doing non-stereotyped work including a farmer, milk delivery person, garage mechanic, bus driver, and the like. One girl was asked to choose the first picture for the book, and she chose the bus driver. The children recognized that the driver was a woman and that she was driving the bus, but they couldn't put it all together because in their perception of the world, women don't drive buses. One girl said, *"She's* a man, right teacher?" The teacher kept asking questions, which helped the children to clarify what they were seeing. The conversation went like this:

T: What is this picture about?
Ch: A bus driver.
T: Who's driving the bus?
Ch: The *lady.*
T: Do you think ladies can drive buses?
Ch: (in chorus) NO!
T: Why not?
Ch: *Ladies* can't drive (Note: These were inner city children who do not often see women driving).
T: *I* can drive a car. But this *lady* is driving the bus. That's her work. Don't you know some ladies who drive cars?
Ch: My daddy can drive but he don't have money for a car.
Ch: I know some ladies who drive cars.
T: I know you don't see ladies driving buses in New York City, but in many other places they do and that is their work.
Ch: Oh!

As the children were talking, the teacher was recording

their comments, and this writer was taping the whole episode. The children's comments changed from incredulous to accepting.

The picture was irrefutable evidence that at least one woman was driving a bus. It would have been a much better experience if this activity could have been followed up by a trip on a bus driven by a woman or by a visit from a female bus driver, but in New York City this was an experience that couldn't be arranged.

The completed book with all the children's comments on this and the other pictures became a favorite in the class library. The teacher backed each page with cardboard, covered them with clear contact, and assembled them in ring binders. The result was a sturdy, useful book.

Later, at a staff meeting, the use of the word lady versus woman was discussed. We pointed out that "lady" is a word with societal connotations that are quite different from "woman," and yet it is often used as a substitute word to mean woman. We suggested that the teachers try to use woman instead but not to purposely "correct" the children when they used "lady." Children learn more by example and, just as teachers try to use correct grammar rather than to correct their grammar, we feel that using non-sexist terms regularly will induce the children to use them also.

The activity described above took place in September. The following April the teacher repeated the same activity. This time two boys and two girls were involved. There was complete acceptance that women can drive. In response to the teacher's question, "Can women drive?" came this answer, "Yeah, some women drive, and the money is also dropping down." The two boys' reactions to a photo of a woman fixing a motorcycle were: "The girl is fixing her motorcycle because it's broken." The teacher asked "Is it hers?" and one boy answered, "Yeah, she rides it. She's fixing it with a screwdriver." The other boy said, "It's a gas woman fixing the motorcycle." The children's comments on a photo of a female letter carrier were, "She is putting a newspaper in a slot that's in the door. It's a mail lady." The teacher replied, "Maybe we could call her a *letter carrier*."

It was evident from the April experience that not only were the children more accepting of the fact that women can and do perform all kinds of tasks, but also that their teacher was actively helping them to develop non-sexist language as well, e.g., "Maybe we could call her a letter carrier?"

Teachers may get some heated denials from their children that men sometimes take care of babies, e.g., pediatric nurses, and that some women are garage mechanics but this is a fine way to begin. Students don't always agree with their teachers, and lively discussion over controversial material is just as appropriate to early childhood as it is to higher levels.

After "Jobs People Do" has become a lively topic of discussion, the next step is to have the children research their families to find out what kind of work various members do. The earliest form of research is to ask someone a question, and even three-year-olds can be expected to remember a question and report the answer in school the next day. (Note: Not *all* threes can do this, but certainly most fours and fives can be expected to.) After the information about the jobs done by the children's families has been collected, teachers will have better ideas about how much further research they must do in the community to provide non-sexist trips and visits for the children.

Trips and Visits A series of visits, trips, and follow-up activities are effective ways to expose children to the world of work. Children as young as three can learn a great deal from having their own mothers, fathers, and other family members come to school to share their expertise. A teacher of threes tried this program:

I decided that the best way to acquaint the children in my class with the fact that many of their mothers were "experts" in various fields was to invite several of them, who did work that was interesting to children, to come and visit and teach or demonstrate their skill. In a class of thirteen three-year-olds, I found among the mothers an opera singer, a horticulturist, a folk singer, and a photographer. I also found a father who was an artist, but he was too shy to share his work with the children.

Each of the mothers spent a part of the morning with us. The horticulturist conducted a whole planting session; the opera singer sang very soft lullabies in several languages during rest time; the photographer took both stills and movies and let the children explore the cameras; and the folk singer conducted a music time for us. The children soon learned that their mommies were "experts" in various fields, and it was an especially rewarding experience because the children already knew these women as the mommies of their friends and learned to view them in another way as well.

This teacher had a fine idea that worked especially well for threes. For fours and fives, we suggest that the idea be. expanded to include fathers and members of the extended family. The jobs such visitors have do not all have to be non-stereotyped. It's far more important that a child's parent or relative is made to feel welcome and that the jobs they do are treated with respect than that they be especially non-stereotyped. It is also extremely important to include men and women who have a special expertise in a homemaking skill, such as baking, cooking, or stitchery, in this study of jobs. We want children to understand that these are also a form of work.

One of the demonstration centers had already developed a pattern of taking small groups of children to visit their parents at work. They visited local factories, stores, and a hospital where many of the parents worked in jobs ranging from aides to physicians. No more than four or five children went on a trip at one time. They could usually walk to their destination, although they sometimes took buses and subways.

We thought this was a fine idea and shared it with our three other centers. They all found it an excellent way to help children understand the work their parents performed while they were at school. The teachers all felt that visits gave the child whose parent was visited a special feeling of sharing. This is especially important to children in day care centers whose parents often cannot take time off from work to attend school functions. The visits also exposed children to a wide variety of jobs. Since each trip generated excitement, each job seemed very special to the children and enhanced their respect for *all* work.

In one school, a mother who is a cab driver arranged to drive by the school at a certain time and let the children see her at work. The children were thrilled by her visit and pored over the cab admiring every part. The mother told the teacher that her own estimation of her work had gone up because of the way the children reacted. Before she had felt a bit ashamed of being a cab driver, but the fact that the teacher had especially asked her to share her work and the children's positive reaction to S—'s mommy driving a taxi made her feel a greater self-respect!

In addition to tapping parents as rich resources of information about jobs, the community offers a wealth of experiences suitable for young children. Teachers will need to do a little research to find out what the school neighborhood has to offer in the way of people performing non-stereotyped jobs. Spreading the word about what one is seeking is helpful. In our centers, parents helped to find many exciting experiences for the children.

When arranging a visit it is usually a good idea to tell the person how long you will stay (keep it short) and suggest the things you think will interest children the most. It's also wise to let them know that short answers to questions are better than long explanations. Usually if the teacher arranges a convenient time for a visit, people are flattered and quite willing to let children come and talk to them.

A fairly simple trip to arrange is to visit a female building superintendent or manager. This is a job that is held by a woman fairly often, but children usually think of it as a man's job. She can explain how she keeps the building warm, how she repairs things that need fixing, and how she keeps the building clean.

Another easily arranged trip is to a local cleaner where a male tailor is employed. Adults know that most tailors are male, but young children associate sewing with females and, for them, seeing a man who sews is a non-sexist experience. Also, tailors are often older men (tailoring is a dying craft), and it adds another dimension to the trip for children to see an older person at work. If it is at all possible to arrange, invite the tailor to come to the children's school and teach them some simple stitchery.

It may be easier for the boys to participate in a stitchery project if it is taught by a man.

As mentioned earlier, because of media and materials, children overwhelmingly view community jobs as male-dominated. This is no longer true; children's perceptions of community jobs can be expanded to include women through a series of trips and visits. Again, teachers will have to do a little prior planning to make sure that female letter carriers and police officers (two favorites of children) are present when the children visit the post office or the police station. If possible, arrange for them to conduct the tour for the children.

In two of our centers, female police officers played a dramatic role in enhancing the children's views of women's strength and the jobs they are able to do. The children in one center walked to the local police station for a visit. They met several male police officers and one female. The female officer spent quite a bit of time answering the children's questions, and both she and the children were delighted to discover that she was assigned to patrol the block where their center was located. They began seeing her on patrol as they came to school, and on occasion they even saw her in the building. She had promised to visit the classroom, and one day she arrived, resplendent in full uniform including her holster, handcuffs, whistle, and walkie-talkie. During her visit she answered all the children's questions and had her picture taken with them. This police officer was a tall, strong, black woman who provided a very positive role model for the black girls in this five-year-old class. One black girl in particular, who had often commented about how she couldn't do this and that and how girls were weak, dramatically changed after the visit of this energetic woman who, in the eyes of the children, did such important work.

In another center, the children had the experience of seeing a female officer on duty daily at the crossing near their school. When she came to visit, the children seemed to accept matter-of-factly that either a man or woman could be a police officer. They showed enormous interest in the paraphernalia of her work, especially the handcuffs, but in no way indicated that they were surprised that she was female. We would consider it ideal if all children could show such lack of surprise at females in community jobs, for that would mean that enough women were so employed that children could view these jobs as performed by *people* rather than by men and a few women.

Another important aspect of community work is medical care—the work of doctors, nurses, dentists, lab workers, technicians, aides, and so on. These jobs become stereotyped very early in the minds of young children, and the stereotypes often prevail even though the child's own situation is contradictory. For instance, many children who have female doctors think that *really* all doctors are male and all nurses are female and shrug off the fact that their own doctor is a woman! No teacher has ever gone through a whole year with pre-schoolers without having to arbitrate the argument that arises when a girl wants to be a doctor and a boy (and sometimes even another girl) challenges her right just because she's a girl. The retort usually goes, "You can't be the doctor—you have to be the nurse 'cause you're a girl."

To help children begin to understand that both men and women can be doctors *and* nurses it would be a good idea to have a pair of each visit the classroom. We feel that it's especially beneficial to have both a male and female who perform the same job come together for a visit, since this reinforces the fact that men and women can do most jobs equally. We designed our community workers block accessories this way and have urged manufacturers to do the same as they develop non-sexist materials.

We feel it is better to have medical workers visit the classroom because hospitals and clinics produce anxiety in so many children. They are more likely to be relaxed and interested if the medical workers visit their own familiar classroom. Of course, some early childhood centers provide medical and dental services, and children become used to clinics. If this is the case, try to arrange to have female dentists and doctors and male nurses and aides work with the children.

One of our centers had an experience with a female dentist that almost hurt our project. When the children went for their regularly scheduled checkup, the director was especially excited because the dentist assigned to them was a woman. However, she was most abrupt and evidenced no special attention or kindness. Indeed, she was almost rough. The director was chagrined and was going to request a different dentist for the follow-up work. She decided to talk to the woman instead and helped her to understand that it was doubly important for her to establish a good relationship with the children, both for the sake of a positive attitude toward tooth care and for the non-sexist project. The woman was understanding on both scores, and the next visit was a much more positive experience for all concerned.

We feel that finding a male nurse is very important in the study of medical workers. Although about 15 percent of nurses are now male, very few children even know that it is possible for a man to be a nurse and most have never seen one. We feel that this is an important option to open up for boys. They should feel that when they begin to look at career choices in their teens, the choice of nursing is one they can make freely, if they are so inclined, without feeling that they are mavericks who are in for a struggle.

Construction work is another job that has special appeal for young children. To "build a building" is an important and powerful job that calls for strength and brains. Needless to say, construction work has been, until very recently, exclusively a male occuption and, as was discussed earlier in the section on block building, the male dominance of building work carries over into the classroom. However, nowadays it is quite possible in most communities to show children that both men and women can build. The number of women architects and engineers is growing every year; one doesn't have to search too hard to find one who will share her work with children. It is also becoming easier to find women carpenters and, although still rare, women laborers.

In New York City our project was able to find a woman building engineer and a woman architect who allowed the children to visit them on building sites and see them on the job in construction clothes. The first experience involved a trip (on a subway) to see a female building engineer who was supervising the building of a bank in the heart of Rockefeller Center. We were doubly pleased about this trip because the husband of one of the teacher aides in the school had seen this woman and had told his wife about her. She in turn told the teacher who then arranged the visit. Before the children went on the trip, they discussed what they were going to see, and one girl especially expressed disbelief that any woman could do such work.

When they arrived at the site, there she was in construction clothes complete with hardhat, supervising a whole group of male workers! The children observed and asked questions, and the teacher took pictures. When they returned to school, the little skeptic burst into the classroom and informed a teacher who had not gone on the trip, "We saw a lady and she was the boss!"

The next day, as a follow-up activity, the teacher set out wood, glue and cardboard, and those children who chose to could "construct." One little girl, who had always said she wanted to be a fireman or policeman, began to build a bank, just as she had seen on the trip. She spent at least one hour building a huge construction, and when it was finished, she took the female construction worker (Women's Action Alliance had given the center a set of its newly designed block accessories containing male and female counterpart community workers) and placed her on top of the building saying, "She's the boss." She then placed the male construction worker near her and said, "He's her helper." Next, she dictated a story to her teacher relating all she had seen the day before and describing the big bank she had just constructed. This was a strong little girl who had experienced something she was very comfortable with—a positive role image of a woman performing a powerful, active job.

Another group took a trip (this time by subway and bus) to see a woman architect who was supervising the development of an entire new town going up on an island in the middle of the East River. The architect showed the children the various types of houses being built and then pointed out one of the oldest buildings in New York, which is being left intact as a landmark. Before they left, she showed them a new playground and let them try some of the equipment. The teacher later described the trip as a "mind boggling" experience that included the wonderful adventure of the transportation they had used to reach the site, especially a train that went under the river!

One more trip, although ordinary, worked out quite extraordinarily one year. The children were taking their usual walk to the firehouse in the fall. When a fireman wanted to dress one of the boys up in the fire fighters' clothes, the teacher pointed out to him that a five-year-old girl was every bit as excited by what she was seeing and suggested that he dress her up instead. He did so and also let her "drive" the fire truck and climb the ladder. The teacher photographed the girl in full fire fighting regalia and also took pictures of her "driving" and climbing. We took the photos, had them enlarged to 8 × 10 inch prints, and made puzzles from them.

Each year after the trip to the fire station, the teacher gave the children a very large carton they would make into a fire truck, and weeks of dramatic play centering around the trip would ensue. This year, spurred by the little girl's excitement and the pictures and puzzles, the girls were much more involved in the dramatic play than they had ever been before. They "drove" the truck, put out fires, and actively participated in painting and designing the truck. The teacher put the words "firegirl" and "firewoman" on the wall alongside "fireboy" and "fireman." (Actually the non-sexist term "fire fighter" would have been preferable.)

Even though these children had never seen a female fire fighter, just a small change in their normal trip was enough to produce noticeable change in their play! In many communities, women are actually actively involved in fire fighting. Even more changes in children's attitudes can be expected when it is possible to give them this kind of first-hand experience.

Many of the follow-up activities to the trips and visits will originate from the children themselves in the form of spontaneous dramatic play, block schemes, drawings, paintings, questions, and so forth. However, teachers will want to plan some activities themselves.

As a natural follow-up activity to the trip to see the building engineer, the teacher had set out building materials and written down dictated stories. Another natural follow-up would have been to plan a block scheme with the children. Planning block building would have helped them to organize their knowledge so that their bank building and its surrounding buildings would recreate to the best of their ability what they had seen the previous day. This planned experience would serve quite a different purpose from spontaneous building; there is room and need for *both* types of experiences in pre-schools.

A collage mural would be another fine way to record a trip. Scraps of construction paper, thin wood, sandpaper, and other materials can suggest the various textures of buildings in the city. A teacher might also make available clay or plasticine as a modeling material for some children to use to reproduce what they had seen on the trip.

Experience charts, class books, individual books, and poems are all effective ways to help children understand and retain their experiences.

Sometimes one media may be more suitable than another to follow up a particular trip, but, in general, all the traditional early childhood mediums of expression are appropriate for a non-stereotyped look at the world of Jobs People Do. Dictating stories or captions to accompany drawings, for instance, is a common activity in kindergartens and day care centers. Here are three stories "written" by preschoolers in California who made worker collages after playing with the materials developed by the Women's Action Alliance:

This is the doctor. She works in an office. She works on people. She makes them a little bit better.

The End.

This is a nurse. He looks at you and then he puts a stick in your mouth to look in it. He takes your temperature then he lets you go home.

The End.

This is a construction worker. She works with the things on the windows in buildings. She can fix buildings.

The End.

Using Photographs Children as well as adults are extremely responsive to photography. They love to see themselves. Recording their trips and visits with photos is not only fun but helps them to recall small details they might otherwise forget. Some older children (some fives and most sixes and sevens) can be trained to use a simple camera and take their own pictures, but it's wise for a teacher, parent, or aide to take some also so that if the children's pictures are not too clear, there will be others to record the trip. The photos can also be used for a variety of follow-up activities. They can be the illustrations for books the children make. They can put one-sentence captions under the photos or tell longer stories that the teacher writes down for them. Since prints are a bit expensive, photos should be used for a book or chart made by the whole group for classroom use rather than in individual books for taking home. For individual books the children can do their own drawings.

Another good use for photos is in a large montage poster titled "Jobs People Do." The children can mount their photos on large pieces of artboard or any large stiff material available and make a poster that records all their trips and visits. This poster can then be used by teachers as a basis for several kinds of discussions revolving around the unit. Sometimes they may want the discussion to be free-wheeling, allowing the children to talk about anything pertaining to jobs. Other times they may want to be more specific and to focus on a particular trip or a specific type of work. Varying discussion from general to specific topics is a good exercise that helps children organize the materials they've learned about a subject. It is also an aid in helping children to learn to speak to the point.

Having some fairly large photos of people at work around the room can stimulate one-to-one discussions between teacher and child or between children. Not every activity has to be planned as long as the classroom environment contains changing stimuli so that the children are challenged to inquire and discuss. Photos are an excellent source of just such inquiry as one teacher relates:

I had seen a telephone company advertisement which featured a little black boy about five years old with tears streaming down his face. I cut it out and hung it up at eye level in my classroom. It was amazing how much conversation ensued. I had a little black boy in my class who cried quite a bit, and he was really able to relate to that picture! Many of the children would look at the picture and when I noticed one doing so, I would wander over and we would start talking about what made us sad. We also discussed why people cry, what made our parents sad, and the like. In short, the picture provided a wonderful catalyst for discussing sadness, an emotion that adults often try to avoid discussing with little children, but one they really need to talk about.

Projects for Older Children Many day care centers and other institutions that care for children have both upper-elementary school children and teen-agers who spend after-school hours at the center. It has been this writer's experience that such schools often have problems programming stimulating experiences for these children.

One suggestion for these after school groups would be to utilize them in the Jobs People Do unit. While young children can go on walking trips in their own communities or even a bit further afield in their exploration of the world of jobs, there are many areas that would be inappropriate or too far away for them to visit. However, children from eleven years and up can make trips into the larger community with still cameras and, if possible, movie cameras to record and bring back information to the younger children. For example, one would not want to take small children into a large hospital complex, nor would they be allowed to visit, but it could certainly be arranged for teen-agers to go to such a place and photograph the enormous variety of jobs performed by men and women. Another example would be to have older children visit a factory or large utility, which would be overwhelming for younger children, and again report their visit photographically.

These older children could prepare movies, filmstrips, slide shows, charts, and verbal presentations for the younger children. Becoming involved in such a project would not only broaden the look at the world of jobs for the younger children, it would also expose teen-agers to job options that they may not have known existed.

Teen-agers need far less adult supervision on trips than younger children, but they do need help in preparing their projects and reports. With adult supervision and guidance about what is relevant and interesting to young children, older children can also gain valuable insights into how young children think and learn, and these will help them become more knowledgeable, understanding, and effective parents.

THE HUMAN BODY

The following ideas for a study of the human body with young children originated in the Resource Room of the Educational Alliance Day Care Center.[2] This is a room where children from the four- and five-year-old groups come (ten at a time) to participate in special projects. The catalyst for much of the unit was a book in the center that was part of the non-sexist materials we were testing. In the words of the center's Director, Anne Gray Kaback, "This is a real breakthrough book!"

The book is *Bodies* by Barbara Brenner (see Annotated Bibliography). It contains photographs of all kinds of bodies doing all kinds of things. Men and women of all ages and children are portrayed actively investigating the world. Whole bodies and parts of bodies are shown. One most important page depicts such essential bodily functions as breathing, eating, moving, sweating, eliminating, and sleeping. There is a photo of two naked little boys playing in a stream and on the facing page one of two little girls playing in a bathtub.

Another page has a picture of a robot with the mechanisms of its insides clearly visible and the following text:

What's a body like?
Is it a machine?
It has parts like a machine.
If you listen hard you hear something ticking inside like a machine.
But . . .
A body is alive.
A machine isn't alive.

2. The teacher in charge of the Resource Room and responsible for the development of this curriculum unit is Ann-Marie Mott.

A machine has no feelings.
So a body can't be a machine even though it seems like a machine.

These few simple questions and statements are rich stimuli with which to introduce children to an area of study that is of prime importance to their development of self-image—the study of their own bodies.

As a matter of fact, the realization that her children did not have a well-developed self-image led Ms. Mott to seek out ways to give her students experiences that would increase their physical self-awareness. She recalled:

I had been wanting to focus on the body since last year. I had asked the children to draw themselves, and their drawings were so incomplete for children their age. It seemed to me that their self-image was poor, in spite of the fact that they were physically capable and well coordinated.

I felt we needed to focus on "Who am I?" We started with handprinting and footprinting. Each child compared the prints of his/her own feet and hands and noticed the similarities and differences between them. Then the children compared their own prints with those of their friends to develop such concepts as smaller and larger, and wider and narrower.

Next, we traced each child's body outline on a large sheet of brown wrapping paper and cut it out. This enabled the children to realize their actual dimensions. There's a big difference between seeing yourself in a mirror and having a life-size cutout to look at and study!

The children filled in the features and painted clothing on the figures and then each of them wrote a story about themselves telling their names, who their special friends were, what they liked to eat, and what they wanted to be when they grew up.

We followed up the brown paper figures by making chalk outlines on the roof. The children traced each other and their teachers, and again they were able to compare relative sizes and shapes. All of these activities took place in the early fall and helped give the children greater understanding of the outer dimensions of their bodies and a sense of greater detail about their extremities.

When the Women's Action Alliance introduced the book *Bodies* into the center, it provided the catalyst for focusing on another dimension, the inner parts of the body and the functions they perform.

The children were fascinated by the book and were especially intrigued by the robot. They wanted to make a robot, which they did, using boxes, scrap machinery, and a battery for the light bulb eyes. Naturally, there was discussion about the connecting parts inside the robot, particularly what connections were necessary to make its eyes light up. The teacher then compared this to the inner workings of the children's bodies and helped them understand that they too had essential inner connections.

After the children made the group robot, they each made an individual robot using boxes, masking tape, egg cartons, and pipe cleaners. Their teacher said of these robots:

They were so fantastically original. Some of the children cut out sections of paper egg cartons and pasted them on for eyes. I had each child make a plan before starting the robot. I felt that this was a good experience for them. They really were able to stick to their plans.

The individual robots were so special I decided to make a book about them. I called the book *Who Made the Robot?* and made it in the following way:

On the left side of the page, each child wrote his or her name and then dictated a robot story to me. I folded the right side of the page less than halfway toward the middle and on the outside flap placed a photo of the child's robot which I had taken and developed. When the right flap was lifted, there was a photo of the child underneath revealing who had made the robot!

In the five-year-olds' classroom, the teacher converted the doll corner into a hospital for the Human Body unit. The children listened to their own and each other's heartbeats with a stethoscope. Both boys and girls created dramatic play situations revolving around health care. The teacher reported that girls felt quite free to be doctors as well as nurses and that both boys and girls were very involved with caring for the sick. Both real children and dolls were the patients.

Next the teachers arranged a trip to the Museum of Natural History so the children could see the transparent woman. This is a life-size figure of a woman made of clear plastic with all of the internal parts of the body clearly visible. In the teacher's words, "The children re-

sponded to the woman with wonder, curiosity, and respect. Those usual embarrassed giggles evoked by pictures of nudity were absent." The children also realized from seeing the woman and from an X-ray photo of a hand in the book *Bodies* that the Halloween skeleton that hung in their room represented the skeletal structure inside their own bodies! As one five-year-old expressed it, "I liked the robot lady [transparent woman] the best because it's important to know about how your body works!"

This gifted teacher thought of still another way to enhance this exciting study of the body for the children.

She arranged a visit to the Central Park Zoo where the children saw the baby gorilla Patty Cake. It was a moving experience for the children to see how similar their bodies were to this young animal and how similar her need for nurturance was to theirs. Observing Patty Cake and her family was an affective experience for the children that, added to the cognitive experiences they had been having, made their study of the body more totally satisfying than if either aspect had been ignored.

In the classroom, the children recreated their visit to Patty Cake and her family in dramatic play situations in which both boys and girls cared for the baby. This play helped them to express their deepest needs and feelings. The children became so involved in this experience that they made lemonade and baked cookies, which they then sold to raise money to make a more natural environment for the gorillas at the zoo!

Songs and rhythms were also part of the body study. For this aspect, Ms. Mott turned to another teacher in the Center who was especially gifted with music. Old standbys such as "Punchinello" and "Looby Loo" helped the children identify parts of their bodies. Other songs used were "Put Your Finger in the Air" and "If You're Happy and You Know It, Clap Your Hands." Ella Jenkins' songs that emphasize the parts of the body were also played. For example, "And One and Two," which appears on the record of the same name (Folkways Records, #7544), combines counting, rhythmic movements, and parts of the body.

The music and games were not new. In fact, they were familiar to both children and teachers. What was new was the focus. When their old favorite songs became a part of the Human Body unit, the children and teachers became more aware of the words and more interested in relating them to their individual bodies.

When the children had been studying the human body for some months, had seen the transparent woman, and made several visits to the zoo to visit Patty Cake and her family (which was important to the family study as well as the human body study), the Alliance staff met with the center's staff for a final in-service session. We all discussed what activities had taken place and how they had brought about changes in the children's self-concepts. All the teachers who had taken part in the unit felt that the children had a new interest in their bodies based on intellectual understanding and curiosity. The teachers and the director noticed far less tittering and toilet talk. As the children found that their questions were answered openly, they no longer needed to sneak and peek. The children also showed pride in their bodies and their knowledge of its functions. The girls were especially delighted that the life-size figure in the museum was female.

HOMEMAKING

In the course of the non-sexist project, the Alliance staff spoke to numerous groups of women who shared with us their concerns and their feelings about the women's movement and the effects it has had on their lives. While many of the women we met were mothers who work outside their homes in paying jobs, many others were women who work as full-time homemakers. Although the women who are full-time homemakers work hard at their jobs of housekeeping and child care, they are not paid any wages and consequently they are regarded as low-status people by our society, which measures jobs mainly by their monetary value. Needless to say, women who are full-time homemakers generally have a poor self-image and when asked what they do, usually say, "I'm *just* a housewife." Very frequently, when one discusses work with young children and asks them what their parents do, they will say, "My mommy doesn't do anything; she just stays home," if their mother is a homemaker.

We feel that homemaking is a complex job that requires a multitude of skills, including executive ability, to handle it successfully. We feel that homemaking is one of *many* work options open to women and that it is as deserving of respect as any job performed in our society. Many women we spoke with who are full-time homemakers feel that the women's movement, with its stress on paid jobs, has left them out. They told us that they feel guilty that they are not using their skills in the outside world, despite the fact that a homemaking career is one they have freely chosen and find satisfying. We feel there is justification for the way these women perceive the messages of the women's movement. Full-time homemaking is not often considered as an option deserving equal status and respect as a paying job.

Also, since homemaking skills are overwhelmingly performed by women and since women don't regard them as skills comparable to those performed by men, they do not often discuss or even think about the complexities of the work they do. Men, who hardly ever experience the complexities involved in running a household smoothly, seldom realize or appreciate the jobs performed by homemakers. They simply take it for granted that their households function properly. On the other hand, the details of performing their own jobs, no matter how menial, are matters for daily discussion, encouragement, and praise.

On the basis of what women told us, we decided that the early childhood classroom would be an appropriate place to begin to look at homemaking as a profession. Although it could be considered a part of the Jobs People Do unit, homemaking is comprised of so many component parts, we decided to present it as a separate unit.

Our hope is that when experience in homemaking skills is provided to young children and these experiences are related to jobs in the world outside the home, children will gain understanding and respect for this work. We also hope that as mothers share their homemaking expertise with their children, as an important part of this study, their own self-esteem will improve.

How to Begin As always, our suggestion is to begin by finding out what children already know. What is their understanding of homemaking? Do they see it as domestic chores only or do any of them perceive that it is more than cleaning, ironing, cooking, and the like?

After finding out what the children's perceptions of homemaking are, a teacher might say, "Let's take a look at the work our mommies do" or, "Homemakers do a big job—let's study about it." We suggest that teachers adopt the term "homemaker" since housewife has negative connotations and also leaves out the occasional man who is a homemaker. Next, break down homemaking into its component parts and relate them to jobs that the children are familiar with in the outside world. For example, food preparation can be compared to the restaurant business; health care can be compared to nursing; the coordinating and planning aspects of homemaking can be compared to the work of a business executive; laundry is done by homemakers and is also a business, and the same thing is true of cleaning.

Meal Preparation An excellent way to help children understand that meal preparation is a complex job that involves budgeting, purchasing, storing, preparing, serving, and cleaning up is to take them to visit a restaurant. Before going on the trip, arrange to have the owner spend a little time with the children and explain the intricacies of the business. Try to arrange the trip when there are no customers in the restaurant so that there will be no danger of the children getting in the way of scurrying waiters and hot food. Make sure the manager explains, very briefly, the many steps required to put meals on the table.

When the children return to their classroom after a restaurant visit, suggest that they pretend to be restauranteurs. Go through all the planning stages that the restaurant owner described. Have the children plan a menu, decide how much they will have to spend, go shopping for the food, cook it, set the table, serve the food, and, finally, clean up. Each child can choose the way she or he would like to participate. Some children can be shoppers, some waiters, some cooks, some customers, and some cleaners. Naturally, all of these activities will not take place on one day as they do in a real restaurant, but over a period of several days. We also do not suggest this complicated activity for children under five.

The final step would be to help the children to understand that their mothers do all this work every time they prepare a meal. One way to do this is to invite one or two mothers to come to school and talk to the children about how they plan their family meals. Perhaps the visiting mothers can help the children to make a classroom chart that lists the various steps of meal preparation. The chart could be illustrated with pictures of shopping, cooking, eating, and cleaning up.

Other follow-up activities can include original stories, experience charts, a large mural of the restaurant the children visited, or of a restaurant they made themselves.

Another possible follow-up activity would be to have children make up a play about their experiences. This would be a more abstract form of pretending than the experiential pretending they did following their visit to the real restaurant.

Health Care-Nursing Since so much of a homemaker's time is taken up with health care, it would be interesting to present this aspect of the job by helping children compare what their mothers do at home to some of the services that nurses perform. A nurse and a mother could be invited to come to school on the same day and demonstrate infant care to the children. This could include how to hold, diaper, bathe, and feed a newborn infant. They could demonstrate with a doll.

A visiting mother could also participate in dramatic play with the children. For example, a child could pretend to be sick, and the visiting mother would pretend to take its temperature, check the symptoms, speak with the doctor, give "medication," and amuse the patient just as a nurse would do.

Another suggestion is to have the visiting mother take care of one of the adults in the room such as the teacher or an aide, since homemakers take care of sick adults too. It would be especially interesting for a male staff member to be a patient, if one is available.

A visiting mother might tell the children a story about how the food she buys is related to health care. She might also talk about vitamins and medicines and stress the fact that she must be an expert on safety so she will know how to protect babies and young children from medicines and other dangerous items in the home.

A final suggestion for relating home health care to nursing is to have both a mother and a nurse demonstrate first-aid techniques. The visitors might show how to put a splint on a sore finger or bandage a sprain or properly disinfect a wound. These are everyday ailments that would not in any way frighten the children.

The nature of these suggestions is dramatic and close to everyday occurrences in the lives of young children, and dramatic play is a spontaneous follow-up activity. It will occur naturally and need little or no teacher direction.

A more structured follow-up activity is for the children to make a large chart with a picture of a homemaker and of a nurse at the top. Brightly colored string, yarn, or ribbon can be attached to them and lead to pictures of the various health care functions the children have learned about. A class book can also record the various health care functions of homemakers.

Household Manager-Business Woman This is a harder concept than the others to get across to young children because it is more abstract. A good way to do it is to ask two women, one who is a homemaker and one who is a business woman, to come and visit together to talk about ways in which their jobs are similar. For example, they could make some charts about their budgets (circular pie wedge charts would be good for this); they can show how they each write checks to pay bills; they can pretend to call up and schedule appointments or order supplies. Perhaps they can both pretend to go to a meeting. For this demonstration, teachers should pick visitors carefully to get women who are at ease pretending, since they will actually be role-playing for the children.

Laundry and Cleaning Doing the laundry and cleaning the home are the most taken for granted chores of a homemaker. When one goes to a commercial laundry and sees the processes involved and the prices charged to clean clothes, or when one pays a high price for a home cleaning service, one realizes that these are time consuming, difficult chores. Through experiential activities a teacher can help children become aware that these

82

aspects of homemaking require skill and strength.

Ask the children if they think doing laundry and cleaning are hard or easy. Also ask them how they think both chores are done. When the children have discussed all they know about these jobs, try to arrange a trip to a laundry and a visit from the maintenance person who cleans the school. After the visits suggest that the children be laundry workers or cleaners also.

On laundry day the teacher might take the children to an automatic laundry if there is one close by. This is really a more relevant way to teach about laundry than having the children do hand washing. However, even if there is no laundry near enough, hand washing will help children to realize that doing laundry is hard work, which is the point of the whole experience. If the children go to a laundromat, they will learn about measuring soap, using bleach, and separating colored clothes, all seemingly minor and simple tasks but necessary ones for successful laundering.

On cleaning day, the children can thoroughly clean their classroom. They can wash all the shelves, polish the wood, sweep and mop the floors, shine the mirrors, and so on. By working thus, they will experience both the fatigue and satisfaction that hard physical labor brings.

The object of arranging experiences involving laundry and cleaning is to relate these experiences to the jobs their mothers do as part of their total jobs as homemakers.

Summarizing the Unit An important part of this unit is to devise activities to help children understand that *all* the areas of homemaking they have explored are also performed in the world of work outside the home. We want children to realize that it takes a most competent person to perform such a wide range of jobs. Some ways to summarize the unit so that these goals are attained are:

☐ Have the children write a class story and illustrate it after each section of the unit. When the unit is completed, bind all the stories together into a big book. Some suggested titles for the book are "Homemakers Do Many Jobs," "The Book about Homemaking," and "What Is a Homemaker?"

☐ After each section of the unit, prepare a large picture chart such as the one described in the health care-nurse section. When the unit is completed, display around the room all the charts with a title tying them together such as "Homemakers have to know how to . . ."

☐ After each section of the unit, have the children make a mural (paint or collage) about the work they have explored. When the unit is completed, tape the mural sections together so that they tell a continuous story about homemaking.

☐ When the unit is completed, invite all the adults who helped explain the various jobs of homemaking to come and have a party with the children. Before the party food is served, ask the visitors to read or tell the children a short story about the day they came to visit and what skill they shared with the children.

☐ Have the children make up poems or songs about the part of the unit they liked best and sing or say them in round robin fashion so all the parts of the unit are mentioned or sung about.

☐ It would be very exciting if a parent or teacher could take movies of each section of the unit and then show it. This would be a fine record and really illustrate the total complexity of the homemaking role. If movies are not possible, a photographic essay of the unit would also be an excellent way to record all the activities. The photos could be used as a discussion starter to help the children remember the entire unit.

If respect for the profession of homemaking is a part of the life of a child, that child will grow up with this respect and bring it into his or her own home as an adult.

SPORTS

Sports are an important element of American cultural life. Even very young children are aware that adults consider sports to be very important. This may not always be a positive attitude, since passive sports watching on the part of parents (fathers in particular) often takes an undue amount of time and attention away from children. Further, the competitive aspect is too often the only one stressed by adults when teaching children about sports. And finally, until very recently sports were almost exclusively male dominated activities, which once again reinforced sexism.

This is no longer true. Women have successfully moved into almost every sport and because of this, it is now possible to introduce a non-sexist study of sports into early childhood classrooms. We feel strongly that a study of sports will be a positive, non-sexist learning experience for the following reasons:

☐ It will give both girls and boys a sense of the importance of good physical development.

☐ It will provide models for active recreation.

☐ It will introduce children to sports that are lifelong skills.

☐ It will provide a balance with sedentary intellectual activities.

In addition, building a love of physical activities and providing appropriate games and exercises will increase the physical strength, coordination, and self-image of both sexes.

How to Begin Hang up a picture of a male and female athlete somewhere in the room where the children will be sure to notice it, or attach the pictures to a flannel board and use them to start a discussion that will be aimed, as always, toward finding out what the children already know and feel about sports. We suggest starting with a non-body contact sport such as tennis, running, or ice skating with which most children will be familiar. Try to relate the initial discussion to what parts of the body the sport uses most and to the fact that one must train to be good at any sport. Stress that both women and men practice hard to become experts and that they do some of the same exercises when they train that children do when they play. For example, teachers can point out that all athletes jump rope to strengthen their legs and improve their coordination and stamina. This should help to dispel the myth that jumping rope is only an appropriate activity for girls. Showing a picture of male figure skaters dancing on the ice will help boys understand that men too can be graceful.

Have the children who have tried the sport being discussed describe how it felt. Feelings have much to do with sports, and they should be stressed from the beginning of the study. After the first discussion, the teacher might suggest that the children ask various family members what sports they like best. Ask the children to bring in pictures of athletes that they find in magazines and newspapers. Set up a bulletin board, wall space, or chart where the pictures can be mounted.

Involving Parents Before beginning the unit or soon after the initial discussion, inform parents about the study either through a short meeting, individually as they pick up their children, or by a notice mailed home. Ask them to help by obtaining copies of *womenSports, Sportswoman* (both of which are devoted entirely to women in athletics), *Sports Illustrated,* which frequently has pictures of female as well as male athletes, or other magazines they find with a sports feature. Explain that the purpose of the study of sports is to foster the goals set forth in the beginning of this unit. Be sure to stress that it is desirable for *both* boys and girls to achieve these goals. Since all parents want optimum development for their children, we feel sure they will cooperate. Parents can also become involved by providing concrete experiences for the children, as will be discussed later.

Pictures and Displays As the children begin to bring in pictures of athletes, it will be interesting to see if they bring in more men than women. If they do, make a point of this and explain that now women are more involved in sports than they used to be. This might be a good time to introduce several issues of *womenSports* and *Sports-woman* and show the children all the sports in which women participate. They will probably be surprised at the variety and will need quite a bit of discussion time to incorporate this more equalized view into their understanding.

After the children have been bringing in pictures for a while, teachers can use them in several other ways besides on a display board. For example, each child can select a favorite picture and dictate a story about it, which can become part of a class book.

Each child can dictate one descriptive sentence as a caption to a picture, and they can be compiled into a class book.

Cut-out pictures from magazines can be used for individual collages, or the whole class can contribute to a sports mural collage.

Sports equipment is very exciting material. Children often bring such items as footballs, basketballs, or baseball hats to school long before they engage in the actual sport. It would be both fun and informative to have a sporting goods display. Children can bring equipment on a rotating basis so if an item is needed at home, it will only be out of service for about a week. Each time a child brings a piece of equipment for the display, she or he can explain its use.

This activity will add to other children's knowledge and help the presenting child learn how to speak to a group. It will also help build skills in deductive reasoning. For example, if a child brings a pair of cleated shoes or a baseball uniform, the children can try to hypothesize about why the cleats are necessary or why the uniform hat is peaked. Their reasoning and any clarification the teacher might add can be recorded on an experience chart. A collection of such charts, illustrated with children's drawings of various pieces of equipment, can be mounted around the room or left on the chart holder so that children are free to review the material on them.

Concrete Sports Experiences As already stated, young children learn best through concrete experience, and it is important to provide them in each area of study. Parents, older children of eight to twelve years, teen-agers, older adults, and other community people can be helpful in providing positive sport experiences.

Ask a man or a woman of any age who enjoys jogging or running as a sport to come during outdoor time and lead the children in this activity. Perhaps you can arrange to meet this individual in a park if there is one near the school, or on the roof, or play yard. If necessary, this sport can even be done in the street—the children can run around the block! Explain very carefully to the children that the emphasis in running or jogging is not on winning a race but on building a strong heart, building strong legs, building stamina, feeling good, and having fun. The visitor can also describe the clothing and shoes worn for running or jogging, emphasizing their comfort and safety functions. A woman who jogs or runs regularly could explain to the children the importance of non-slippery shoes. Such an explanation can do much to help a little girl who wants to wear party shoes to school every day to understand why they are both restricting and dangerous!

Many pre-schoolers go ice skating, and they all seem to enjoy the experience. To make skating into a non-sexist sport experience, try to arrange to have a man who figure skates demonstrate his skills. Teachers may have to arrange a trip to a local ice rink or outdoor pond that is thickly frozen in the winter. The most ideal experience would be for the man to "dance" with each child for a few minutes, but if this is not possible, the children can watch him dance a short solo. He can briefly explain the equipment he uses and show the children what exercises he does to keep himself in good skating condition. Perhaps, if each child cannot skate with him, he can lead them all in some warm-up exercises. Another point he should stress is *the good feeling* he gets from skating.

Baseball is usually the first professional sport that children learn about. Until recently small boys had role models of older boys emulating major league teams in Little League or in less organized community teams. In 1973–74 this writer saw little girls going out in groups to play baseball, and, of course, with the court ruling against the male exclusivity of Little League, many more girls will be playing this game.

A good way to introduce younger boys and girls to baseball or softball is to have older children demonstrate it. As with running, this can be done just about anywhere outdoors. A park would be ideal, but a yard or roof will also do. Explain to the older children that you want to show the class that baseball is a game to be enjoyed by both boys and girls. Ask them to show how they bat, run, slide, throw, and catch and then arrange to let each child try to hit a very slowly and closely pitched ball and run around the bases. Encourage the demonstrators to stress the fun and not the competitive aspects of the game.

After the younger children have tried running and batting, one girl and one boy can tell why they enjoy the game. The older children can also explain why they wear special shoes, gloves, hats, or other clothing when they play.

The teacher will have to hold a planning meeting with the older children so that they will learn how to most effectively explain baseball to children younger than themselves. They will need to know that they may have to hold some children's hands as they go around the bases and that some may not be ready to try any part of the activity. We feel that activities such as this help older children gain understanding about the feelings, learning styles, and levels of development of younger children. Such experiences as "teachers" assist older children to grow up to be adults with greater insight into both themselves and children.

Games and Activities Many of the usual outdoor activities that develop coordination and build large muscle strength and control can be done in the context of a sports program. All that is needed is a little more planning for and encouragement on the part of teachers. We certainly are not advocating turning outdoor time into a highly structured activity where children are not free to choose their own play. We do suggest adding some of the following as one of the free choices available during outdoor time.

Have one teacher or aide lead a ten-minute exercise period in the yard. It can include jumping, bending, running, and the like. Make jump ropes available and encourage boys as well as girls to try. Very young children can simply walk over or under the rope.

Arrange a pitching game either with a ball or bean bag and a wastebasket or box. This old standby game is often neglected now, but it is an excellent builder of coordination and muscle control.

Encourage all the children to use the climbing equipment by relating it to growth and development of strength.

Although sports are mainly physical activities, many language arts experiences can complement the study. Besides classroom books containing the children's original stories or one line captions, which were suggested earlier, teachers can add vocabulary, poetry, stories, and songs relating to sports.

Many words relating to sports and sports equipment will be new to the children, e.g., cleat, jogging, figure skating, and calisthenics. Picture charts with a word clearly illustrated as well as written will help children learn the look and meaning of that word. Using the correct term when discussing an activity will help make the new vocabulary a natural addition to words the children already know. New words are always fun for children, and long ones are especially exciting.

One of the strongest emphases in this unit should be on the feelings that are part of a sports experience. Poetry is an excellent medium for expressing such feelings. The children can start out with simple rhyming games, word plays, and nonsense rhymes that are fun and relaxing. For example, cleat can be rhymed with words that have meaning such as bleat and pleat, but can also be rhymed with nonsense words such as mleat or nleat.

After children have had some practice with simple rhyming, teachers can read them poems that describe feelings and then ask the children to express how *they* feel when they run, skate, slide, or throw a ball. Poetic phrases should come out of this exercise, and teachers can record the children's words. Poems can be made either by combining several of the children's work or individually if a child is very verbal. It does not matter if the poems rhyme—the expression of feeling is what counts.

Be sure to share the children's sports poetry with parents. It will help them understand the goals of the project.

Stories related to pictures have already been discussed, but children will also have stories to tell that relate to the concrete sports experiences they are having. Again, round-robin stories or individual ones can be added to the class library or put on experience charts conveniently located in the room so that children are free to browse among them.

Songs about skating, running, swimming, and other sports can by made up by the children or teachers. The children's poetry can be sung to a familiar tune during music time.

Summary We feel strongly that it is important to bring sports into the *educational* experience of children so that their most positive aspects can be emphasized. We see sports as a way to help children develop physically as well as socially and emotionally. If teachers introduce sports into the classroom as activities that are pleasurable for both girls and boys and provide role models of both women and men who enjoy sports, either as amateurs or professionals, they will set a non-sexist attitude from the beginning. In this way the destructive conditioning that makes girls feel that loving sports conflicts with being "feminine" can be avoided.

We feel very strongly that parents should be included in the study. They need to be helped to understand that girls should participate equally with boys in physical development. They will need to be made aware of the sexist messages little girls are given about sports and how this closes off options for them.

Finally, our stress throughout the study of sports is on the full physical development, positive social experiences, and individual joy that sports can offer, *not* their competitive aspects.

6 Non-sexist Materials

As stated earlier, it became apparent in the observation period of the project that a very necessary part of the work would be to develop non-sexist early childhood materials. We had to hand-produce these materials because none were available and it would have taken too long to launch the program had we waited for them to be produced commercially. We are pleased to report that there are now several items available made from our original designs as a direct result of our efforts with two major manufacturers of early childhood equipment—The Milton Bradley Co. and The Instructo Corp., a division of McGraw-Hill.

All of the materials we produced are early childhood staples, i.e., puzzles, lotto, flannel boards, and block accessories. We feel that these traditional items are useful classroom materials that help children develop important skills. However, at the beginning of the project, our quarrel with these traditional materials was that they were so sexist, outmoded, and stereotyped in their design and format that their usefulness was seriously curtailed.

To combat these deficiencies, the materials we developed not only equalize the work and family roles of men and women, but they also reflect the rich multiracial and ethnic makeup of our society, the variety of sizes and shapes of people, and contemporary hairstyles and dress.

The following commercially made, non-setreotyped, multiracial materials are now available:

92

BLOCK ACCESSORIES

Our Community Helpers Play People This set contains
twelve male and female workers in counterpart community jobs. Included are letter carriers, construction workers,
doctors, nurses, police officers, and business executives.
These figures are suitable for dramatic play in conjunction
with block building and can also be used in a variety of
ways in the Jobs People Do unit. They are also usable as
puppets if a stick is attached. (Manufactured by The Milton
Bradley Co.; distributed by the Women's Action Alliance,
370 Lexington Ave., New York, N.Y. 10017.)

My Family Play People The set consists of two families,
one white and one black. Each contains six figures: two
parent-aged people, a young child, a young adult, and two
older people. The females in this set do *not* wear aprons
or have babies painted in their arms! Children are free
to use the figures to represent the reality of their own
families, rather than being confined by the nuclear family concept normally found in children's materials. Both
the black and white family figures are packaged in one
set; this provides the opportunity for children from an
interracial family to pick from the dozen figures those
that most closely represent the members of their own families. For the same reason, the set provides material for
children who live in interracial neighborhoods. Both sets
of block accessories are drawn with great detail and are
complete front and *back*. (Manufactured by The Milton
Bradley Co.; distributed by the Women's Action Alliance,
see address above.)

Community Careers Flannel Board The set contains
twenty-seven figures of men and women dressed in appropriate work clothes or uniforms. As in the other materials,
men and women represent a wide variety of community
jobs, sometimes in counterpart roles. The set also contains props that are appropriate to the various jobs. This
material can be used by teachers to illustrate jobs in the
Jobs People Do unit. It can also be used by an individual
child or a small group of children. (Manufactured by The

Instructo Corp.; distributed by the Women's Action Alliance, see address above.)

PHOTOGRAPHS

People at Work This set consists of twenty-four 8 × 10 inch black and white photos of people at work. Men and women have been photographed on location doing their jobs. An effort has been made to find as many non-stereotyped workers as possible. This is a valuable resource for the Jobs People Do unit as it shows boys and girls the enormous variety of options that are open to them in the world of work. The photography was done by Jolly Robinson and Ann-Marie Mott. (Manufactured by The Instructo Corp.; distributed by the Women's Action Alliance, see address above.)

Resource Photos of Men in the Nurturing Role This set consists of eight 8 × 10 inch black and white photos of men interacting with young children. There are fathers, grandfathers, and men who work with children as teachers and pediatric nurses. Also included is a poster featuring a grandfather and granddaughter in a group of sequential photographs involving playing with grandpa's hat. This poster is ideally suited to a variety of language arts activities. These photos are an asset to both the Families and Jobs People Do units. Photography by Jim Levine. (Distributed by the Women's Action Alliance, see address above.)

Resource Photos of Women in Community Jobs and in Professional Roles These are two separate sets of photos containing eight 8 × 10 inch black and white pictures each. The community set is especially good and contains a milk deliverer, a letter carrier, a police officer, and a bus driver. The professional set is not quite as good because some of the professions are a bit hard to define, e.g., a politician and a computer programmer, but others such as a judge and a potter are fine. The sets are quite inexpensive and are a valuable resource. (Distributed by

Feminists for Equal Education, Box 185, Saxonville Station, Framingham, Mass. 01701.)

Other Photos When we began to develop non-sexist materials in 1972, we relied heavily on advertising photos. Whenever we saw an ad in a magazine that would be useful in a non-sexist curriculum, we cut out as many as we could find and then wrote or phoned the advertiser to ask for reprints, which they were always willing to send. Currently there are many ads around featuring fathers and young children. Fathers are shown holding the children, reading to them, and generally in nurturant poses. It is much easier to build a non-sexist picture file now than it was several years ago. It is also becoming easier to find advertising photos showing women on jobs. Recently ads have appeared portraying a female barber, marine biologist, and garage mechanic.

Your local hospital is a probable source of photos of male and female medical workers. If you call the public relations department, it will usually send photos from its files. It is important to stress that the pictures are for classroom use with young children; otherwise some frightening surgical scenes may be sent.

Ebony and *Essence* magazines are good sources of pictures of black people both at home and at work.

And, of course, a valuable source of photographs is your own school or community. There is certain to be at least one member in your school or community who is a photography buff. This person can be recruited to take pictures for use in the various units.

Pictures of people in the community are especially important to minority groups who are not usually featured in national advertising or other media. For example, if your school is located in a community that is Mexican-American or native American, the children will be exposed through such photographs to role models from their own group and will identify more strongly with them.

And don't forget teen-agers. Many of them are interested in photography and, if asked, will probably be delighted to take pictures of people doing their jobs in the community. Finally, newspapers have been publishing more and more features on women at work, girl and women athletes, and nurturing men. Such articles are excellent sources of unusual pictures.

PUZZLES

The Women's Action Alliance designed several puzzles for the project. These were developed to counteract the commercial puzzles that often picture highly stereotyped or unrealistic cartoon-like animal subjects. We made two puzzles that showed men and women doing non-stereotyped work, three or four of fathers in a nurturing role, and two showing girls in active play.

To date, these puzzles have proved too expensive to be mass manufactured. However, similar ones are relatively easy to make. Here is the method we used to make puzzles:

1. First, select a picture that is non-sexist. Magazine illustrations are excellent for puzzles because the paper is fairly thin, but you can also use photographs successfully.

2. Cut out the picture and cover any advertising print with a scrap piece of paper. When you laminate the picture onto wood, this patch will hardly show.

3. Measure the photo and then measure and cut a piece of wood exactly the same size. The wood can be thin or thick, but it should be easy to cut with a jigsaw.

4. Make a tray into which the wood fits comfortably so children can remove the pieces easily.

5. Laminate the picture onto the wood. We used a sealing material called Decoupage, but if this is not available in your local art supply or hardware store, ask the owner to recommend a similar thin, sealing substance. We applied six coats of Decoupage and rubbed each coat down with fine sandpaper when it was thoroughly dry (it dries very quickly).

6. After the picture is laminated to the wood, turn the wood over and draw an interlocking jigsaw design on

the back. When you draw the design, be careful that all parts of the body are left whole (for example, don't have an arm in two pieces or cut a head in half) and that you make right angle pieces to fit the four corners of the tray.

7. Finally, cut the design with a jigsaw, sand and seal all the rough edges, and your puzzle is ready!

You can also make puzzles from photos of the children or members of the community. Some suggested subjects for puzzles are: people at work (non-stereotyped jobs), men, teen-age boys, and older people caring for children, boys playing with dolls and women and girls engaging in sports. We stress these subjects, not because we don't want puzzles showing boys in active play or women nurturing children or male athletes, but because such puzzles are easy to buy commercially and the subjects we suggest are not.

There are three puzzles commercially available that we do recommend:

Dressing and Undressing This puzzle features a boy and girl of the same size. They each have a fishing net and are sharing a jar of fish they have caught. All their clothing comes off and underneath their genitals are drawn in a very tasteful and childlike way. The puzzle is saying that the real difference between boys and girls is a biological one. (Available from Childcraft Education Corp., 20 Kilmer Rd., Edison, N.J. 08817.)

Crossing Guard This is a multiracial puzzle of a woman dressed in uniform and children crossing a street. Although it is called crossing guard, the woman does not have a white crossing guard band across her uniform, but she does have two badges and could be called a police officer. (Available from Judy Puzzles, subsidiary of General Learning Corp., Morristown, N.J. 07960.)

Doctor Part of the Occupation Series (the rest is highly stereotyped). This puzzle features a woman doctor examining a small girl as her mother looks on. The figures are not very well drawn, but it is the only puzzle of a female doctor we have been able to find! (Available from Judy Puzzles, see address above.)

LOTTO GAMES

Lotto games are important for young children. Even three-year-olds can play them successfully and enjoy them. However, commercially produced lotto games are quite stereotyped, and the style of the drawings is very old fashioned.

We made a photographic lotto called Children at Play Lotto, which showed girls *and* boys at play instead of girls watching boys at play, as is usually the case. Play Scenes Lotto is now commercially available. (Manufactured by the Milton Bradley Co.; distributed by the Women's Action Alliance, see address above.) Or you can make your own:

1. Begin by taking enough photographs to make a good selection of thirty-six shots of girls and boys at play. Make sure you have plenty of action shots of girls. Be sure to seek out children of different races too. We took ours in two parks, a school, and a day care center.

2. Have the pictures made into 3×5 inch prints with white borders (the white borders serve as a natural divider between pictures). You will need *two* copies of each print, one for the cards and one for the matching picture. We used color prints, but black and white would do.

3. Buy some sturdy artboard in an art supply shop. Artboard comes in a variety of thicknesses, and you will have to choose what thickness you like best and what your budget can afford. We used artboard about ¼ inch thick so that it had a spongy feeling.

4. Group your pictures according to the type of play. We had a ball playing card, a toddler card, an ice skating card, a running card, a gymnastics card, and a playground card in our set.

5. Choose six pictures for each card and mount them onto

the artboard with liquid cement. Trim the artboard so that the edges of the pictures are flush with the edge of the board.

6. Seal the pictures to the artboard with self-adhesive clear plastic that can be purchased inexpensively at any art supply store.

7. Mount the second print of each photo to an individual piece of artboard and seal it also. This makes the matching set of cards that the children place over the pictures on their boards until their whole board is covered.

We made our lotto Children at Play, but one can make Job Lotto, Family Lotto, Sports Lotto, and so forth, in exactly the same way.

RECORDS

Chock-full of good material that can be used to trigger many non-sexist musical experiences is the recording, *Free to Be You and Me*. The record parallels the book of the same title, edited by Francine Klagsbrum (see Annotated Bibliography). Much of the humor and quite a few of the stories are too sophisticated for younger children, but all of the music is delightful and the words of the songs can be used in the various subject units. For example, "Parents are People" would be an excellent addition to the units on Families and Jobs People Do. Children have always accepted the fact that fathers, but *not* mothers, combine a career with the job of parenting. The song puts working and parenting on an equal basis for mothers and fathers and, in addition, cites many interesting and non-stereotyped jobs performed by both sexes.

"Brothers and Sisters" conveys the type of friendship we would like to see become the norm for boys and girls. The song is joyful, and the kind of feelings that the word brotherhood usually brings to mind—sharing and loving—are expressed here as both sisterhood *and* brotherhood!

Free to Be You and Me states the theme of the record and of our project as well—that is, that children must be free to choose for themselves from life's multitude of options, unhampered by sex-role stereotyping. As is all the music on the record, the song is a joyous ode to freedom.

The poem "I Hate Housework," spoken by Carol Channing, is a hilarious spoof on television commercials that try to make household chores into the world's most satisfying work. Although we wish the title were different, the message of the poem is an excellent way to help children begin to look at TV critically.

"It's All Right to Cry" is a *most* important song because it is about letting out one's feelings, even if they're sad or bad ones. It's especially sung to little boys by Roosevelt Grier.

There are many other parts of the record that can be used in a variety of activities. Teachers will want to pick the poems and songs that have the most meaning and suggest the most program ideas. The children will also pick their favorite parts and sing and dance to the songs and say the poems over and over. (Available from Bell Records. Division of Columbia Pictures Industries, Inc., 1776 Broadway, New York, N.Y. 10019. The record is sold in many outlets or by mail through *Ms. Magazine,* 370 Lexington Ave., New York, N.Y. 10017.)

A TV special, also titled *Free to Be You and Me,* has been made into a film. It is available in its entirety (40 minutes) or as three fifteen-minute segments. (Available from McGraw-Hill Text Films, Dept. SF, 1221 Avenue of the Americas, New York, N.Y. 10020.)

Caedmon Records (505 Eighth Ave., New York, N.Y. 10018) has issued a fine non-sexist record for children from pre-kindergarten–grade six, Hurray for Captain Jane. In it Tammy Grimes reads stories from such books as *Martin's Father* and *Jellybeans for Breakfast.*

DOLLS

After the Alliance's project was well underway, we became aware that Creative Playthings (Princeton, N.J. 08540) had expanded its Sasha line of dolls to include several boy dolls dressed to look like typical four- or five-year-old boys at play. We especially liked the black boy, Caleb, and purchased him for all our centers. Although he isn't a soft doll, he has an unusually smooth finish. Another Sasha doll is called Black Baby and is also very smooth and has a realistic shape. Caleb became very popular with the boys in our centers, and he made it easier for several boys to move into doll play more comfortably.

FILMSTRIPS

While not specifically designed as non-sexist materials, Scholastic has two filmstrip sets that are unusually sensitive portrayals of a wide variety of family life styles. *Five Families* shows youngsters how children live in a Chinese, Mexican-American, native American, black, and white family. *Five Children* shows how children live in various geographic locations. Both *Five Families* and *Five Children* are available in Spanish and English. (Available from Scholastic Early Childhood Center, 904 Sylvan Ave., Englewood Cliffs, N.J. 07632.)

Scholastic's "Beginning Concepts" series, numbers three and four, consist of ten sound/color filmstrips. Entitled *People Who Work,* they depict women and men performing unusual and non-traditional jobs.

ADDITIONAL RESOURCES

The following are useful resources for additional information and materials for non-sexist education. (See also the two bibliographies in the Appendices.)

Publishers
FEMINIST PRESS, Box 334, State University of New York, Old Westbury, N.Y. 11568
Non-sexist books, bibliographies, resource booklets, curriculum materials, and the like.

LOLLIPOP POWER, INC., P.O. Box 1171, Chapel Hill, N.C. 27514
Non-sexist pre-school picture books.

Films and Slides
ODEON FILMS, INC., 1619 Broadway, New York, N.Y. 10019

Producers of *Sugar and Spice*, a film on non-sexist pre-school education.

RESOURCE CENTER ON SEX ROLES IN EDUCATION, Attn. Dr. Shirley McCune, 1156 15th St., N.W., Suite 918, Washington, D.C. 20005

Images of Males and Females in Elementary School Textbooks, prepared by Lenore J. Weitzman and Diane Rizzo, Department of Sociology, University of California at Davis.

WOMEN ON WORDS AND IMAGES, P.O. Box 2163, Princeton, N.J. 08540

Rents a slide show, *Dick and Jane as Victims*, which documents sexism in children's readers. Also sells a pamphlet by the same name. It has prepared a study recently on sexism in children's television entitled *Channeling Children: Sex Stereotyping on Prime Time TV.*

Bibliographies
CHANGE FOR CHILDREN, 2588 Mission St., Suite 226, San Francisco, Calif. 94110

In addition to an excellent bibliography of pre-school books, it has a pamphlet of curriculum ideas and a series of fine photos of women in non-traditional jobs.

FEMINISTS ON CHILDREN'S MEDIA (Distributed by Feminist Book Mart, Inc., 41–17 150th St., Flushing, N.Y. 11355)

It has recently updated its excellent bibliography of non-sexist children's books, *Little Miss Muffet Fights Back.*

THE LIBERTY CAP, 1050 Newell Rd., Palo Alto, Calif. 94303

A monthly bibliographic newsletter of recently published non-stereotyped children's books and resources.

Bookstores
CHILD'S PLAY, 226 Atlantic Ave., Brooklyn, N.Y. 11201

One of the best collections of non-sexist children's books to be found. It sells through mail order and has a catalog.

FEMINIST BOOK MART, INC., 41–17 150th St., Flushing, N.Y. 11355

Another good place to send for non-sexist books.

Resource Centers

RESOURCE CENTER ON SEX ROLES IN EDUCATION, National Foundation for the Improvement of Education, 1201 16th St., N.W., Washington, D.C. 20036

A national center for the dissemination of information on non-sexist education, K-12.

WOMEN'S ACTION ALLIANCE, 370 Lexington Ave., New York, N.Y. 10017

Distributes non-sexist materials and information.

Appendices

ANNOTATED BIBLIOGRAPHY
OF NON-SEXIST PICTURE BOOKS
(See also Non-Sexist Materials Chapter)

Birnbaum, Al. *Green Eyes*. New York: Western Publishing Co., 1953. All about a cat's first year of life. A story of growth, changing seasons, and discovery.

Brenner, Barbara, with photographs by George Ancona. *Bodies*. New York: E. P. Dutton, 1973. All kinds of bodies doing all kinds of things. It shows boys and girls in the nude, and on the page showing bodily functions, it has a photo of a small boy on the toilet. A real breakthrough book!

Brownstone, Cecily. *All Kinds of Mothers*. New York: Mc-Kay, 1969. An interracial book showing mothers who work both outside and inside the home. The common thread is their love for their children.

Burton, Virginia Lee. *Katy and The Big Snow*. Boston: Houghton Mifflin, 1943. Katy is a tractor who is strong enough to plow out an entire snowed-in city.

Hartin

Cohen, Miriam, illustrated by Lillian Hoban. *Will I Have a Friend?* New York: Macmillan, 1967. A little boy on his first day at a child care center (taken there by his father) asks if he will find a friend at school. He begins the day feeling uncertain, but by the time he leaves, he's found many friends and feels more

104

secure. He shows that boys have feelings of uncertainty and that a father can take part in his child's life.

Ehrlich, Amy, paintings by C. A. Porker. *Zeek Silver Moon.* New York: Dial Press, 1972. This exquisitely illustrated book shows the spontaneous affection and humor between father and child. Zeek's father makes him a cradle and sings him a lullaby he made up.

Martin

Eichler, Margrit, illustrated by Bev Magennis. *Martin's Father.* Chapel Hill, N.C.: Lollipop Power, 1971. This very simple story is about a nurturing father. It shows Martin and his father performing all the housekeeping tasks essential to daily life as well as enjoying play situations together. Although it never specifically states that no mother is present in the family, it can be used as a story with which one-parent children can identify. The fact that the nurturing parent in this case is the father makes this book a fine addition to a non-sexist booklist.

Felt, Sue. *Rosa-Too-Little.* New York: Doubleday, 1950. A story of competence and achievement with a little girl as the main character. Rosa wants a library card and has to learn to write her name to get one. She perseveres all summer and achieves her goal. It has fine pictures of summer in the city, and since Rosa is Puerto Rican, it has the added attraction of being a success story about a minority child.

Gaeddert, Lou Ann. *Noisy Nancy Norris.* New York: Hale, 1965. Nancy is inventive and noisy. She finds out her noisiness is not always appreciated.

————. *Noisy Nancy and Nick.* New York: Doubleday, 1970. Noisy Nancy and her new friend, Nick, explore the noisy city together.

Gauch, Pat, drawings by Shimeon Shemin. *Grandpa & Me.* New York: Coward, McCann and Geoghegan, 1972. A young boy recounts his intimacy with his grandpa and their shared love of nature.

Goldreich, Gloria, and Goldreich, Esther. *What Can She Be?* New York: Lothrop, Lee & Shepard, 1972. Photographs show a female veterinarian taking care of animals in her hospital. Two other "What Can She Be?" books portray the work of a broadcaster and a lawyer.

Goodyear, Carmen. *The Sheep Book*. Chapel Hill, N.C.: Lollipop Power, 1972. A story of a farmer and *her* sheep. About life on a California farm.

Hazen, Nancy. *Grownups Cry, Too*. Chapel Hill, N.C.: Lollipop Power, 1973. A simple explanation of the kinds of experiences, both sad and happy, that make men and women and boys and girls cry.

Kaufman, Joe. *Busy People and How They Do Their Work*. New York: Golden Press, 1973. Although the ratio of jobs is five male and three female, two of the female jobs are non-stereotyped. All of the job descriptions are simple and accurate. While not everything in this book is non-stereotyped, there are pictures of a boy and girl roller skating together, male and female telephone operators, and male and female postal workers.

Klagsbrun, Francine, ed. *Free to Be You and Me*. New York: McGraw-Hill, 1974. While many of the stories may be too old for pre-schoolers, the book contains the music for all the songs on the record. Young children will also enjoy some of the poems.

Leaf, Munro, illustrated by Robert Lawson. *The Story of Ferdinand*. New York: Viking Press, 1936. This classic story is about a non-stereotyped bull! He is gentle, quiet, peace loving, and fond of flowers. He does not like to fight, charge, or roar, but he is still a great big, strong bull. It is a fine non-sexist book because it subtly criticizes prescribed roles.

Merriam, Eve, illustrated by Beni Montresor. *Mommies at Work*. New York: Knopf, 1961. A good book about mothers who work *outside the home*. It has a positive tone and combines well the homemaking and working qualities of women. It also depicts many interesting jobs held by women.

————, illustrated by Harriet Sherman. *Boys & Girls, Girls & Boys*. New York: Holt, 1972. Though by the same author, this book is not as successful as *Mommies at Work*. It has merit in that it shows boys and girls who are friends with each other; it depicts children of several ethnic groups; and it shows children with a wide variety of interests that are not sex-typed. The illustrations are often crowded and confusing, and at times the children are almost grotesque. However, it shows both boys and girls hugging soft toys in bed, catching bugs and worms, and helping with household chores.

Miles, Betty, and Blos, Joan. *Just Think*. New York: Knopf, 1971. Shows mothers who work outside the home, fathers enjoying their children, girls in action, and many other realistic and exciting facets of life.

Reavin, Sam. *Hurrah for Captain Jane*. New York: Parents Magazine Press, 1971. While in the bathtub, Jane fantasizes about being the first woman captain of an ocean liner.

Schick, Eleanor. *City in the Winter*. New York: Macmillan, 1970. Jimmy stays with his grandma while his mother goes to work. They spend a long snowbound day together doing a variety of things, such as cooking soup, making a barn out of a box, and feeding the birds.

Sonneborn, Ruth. *I Love Gram*. New York: Viking Press, 1971. A sensitive story about a young girl's love for her grandmother and her fear and sense of loss when Gram gets sick and is hospitalized. It is also the story of a minority home, headed by a working mother.

Surowiecki, Sandra Lucas. *Joshua's Day*. Chapel Hill, N.C.: Lollipop Power, 1972. Joshua lives in a one-parent home. His mother, who is a photographer, drops him off each morning at a day care center where he interacts with both boys and girls.

Thayer, Jane. *Quiet on Account of Dinosaur*. New York: Morrow, 1964. A fantasy about a little girl who finds a dinosaur on the way to school. She learns so much about dinosaurs that she grows up to be a famous scientist.

Van Woerkom, Dorothy, illustrated by Paul Galdone. *The Queen Who Couldn't Bake Gingerbread*. New York: Parents Magazine Press, 1975. An amusing retelling of an old German fairy tale. Both the king and the queen learn about choosing a mate for her or his inner qualities rather than looks. They also learn to do for themselves and to be considerate of each other.

Waber, Bernard. *Ira Sleeps Over*. Boston: Houghton Mifflin, 1972. Ira would like to take his teddy bear to his first sleepover but is afraid his friend will think him a baby. When Reggie takes his teddy out of a drawer, Ira goes home (next door) to get his too. Shows that boys also need the comfort of stuffed animals.

Wolde, Gunilla. *Tommy Goes to the Doctor*. Boston: Houghton Mifflin, 1972. Tommy does to his teddy bear what his doctor (a woman) does to him.

————. *Tommy and Sarah Dress Up*. Boston: Houghton Mifflin, 1972. Two very young friends have a fine time dressing up and try on both male and female clothing.

Yashima, Taro. *Crow Boy*. New York: Viking Press, 1955. Another classic children's book, which belongs on every non-sexist list. *Crow Boy* deals with the feelings of a young boy, a subject not usually dealt with in stories for young children. Chibi is the butt of all the class jokes for six years in elementary school until a male teacher takes the time to discover his uniqueness as a person. By letting Chibi display his unusual talent, he helps the children to realize that they never bothered to find out what kind of person Chibi was, just because he was a little different. A further asset of *Crow Boy* as a non-sexist book is that it is set in another culture, rural Japan. It also teaches the appreciation of difference. Best for children five years and older.

Young, Miriam. *Jellybeans for Breakfast*. New York: Parents Magazine Press, 1968. Two little girls imagine all the fantastic things they will do someday, including going to the moon.

Zolotow, Charlotte, pictures by Ben Schecter. *The Summer Night*. New York: Harper & Row, 1974. A gentle story of a nurturant father and his little girl. When she can't go to sleep on a warm summer night, her dad figures out all sorts of ways they can enjoy themselves.

————, illustrated by William Pene DuBois. *William's Doll*. New York: Harper & Row, 1972. This well-written book is outstanding for both the quality of its language and its message. It is about a boy who wants a doll to nurture, and about the reactions of his family and friends to his request. When the grandmother explains to William's father her reasons for buying William the doll he wants, she gives a moving account of the importance of the development of gentle and nurturing qualities in prospective fathers.

BIBLIOGRAPHY OF SELECTED NON-SEXIST READINGS
(See also Non-sexist Materials Chapter)

Ahlum, Carol, and Fralley, Jacqueline M. *Feminist Resources for Schools and Colleges*. The Clearinghouse on Women's Studies, The Feminist Press, Box 334, Old Westbury, N.Y. 11568, 1973.

Aldous, Joan. "Children's Perceptions of Adult Role Assignment: Father Absence, Class, Race and Sex Influence," *Journal of Marriage and the Family*, vol. 34, no. 1, February 1972, pp. 55–65.

Bem, Daryl J., and Bem, Sandra L. *Training the Woman to Know Her Place: Beliefs, Attitudes and Human Affairs*. Belmont, Calif.: Brooks/Cole, 1970.

Biller, H. B. *Father, Child and Sex Role*. Lexington, Mass.: D. C. Heath, 1971.

Burr, Elizabeth, and others. *Guidelines for Equal Treatment of the Sexes in Social Studies Textbooks*, "The Language of Inequality," pp. 5–12. Westside Women's Committee, P.O. Box 24D20, Los Angeles, Calif. 90024, 1973.

Claven, S. "Women's Liberation and the Family," *Family Coordinator*, vol. 19, 1970, pp. 317–23.

Densmore, Dana. *Speech Is a Form of Thought*, KNOW, Inc., P.O. Box 10197, Pittsburgh, Pa. 15232, 1970.

Emma Willard Task Force on Education. *Sexism in Education*, second ed. rev. Box 14229, University Station, Minneapolis, Minn. 55408, 1972.

Epstein, R., and Liverant, S. "Verbal Conditioning and Sex-role Identification in Children," *Child Development*, vol. 34, 1963, pp. 99–106.

Fasteau, Marc F. *The Male Machine*. New York: McGraw-Hill, 1974.

Fauls, L. B., and Smith, W. D. "Sex-role Learning of Five Year Olds," *Journal of Genetic Psychology*, vol. 89, 1965, pp. 105–17.

Federbush, Marcia. *Let Them Aspire: A Plea and Proposal for Equality of Opportunity For Males and Females in the Ann Arbor Public Schools*. 2000 Anderson Court, Ann Arbor, Mich. 48104, 1971.

Feminists on Children's Media. "A Feminist Look at Children's Books," *School Library Journal*, vol. 18, 1971, pp. 19–24.

———. *Little Miss Muffet Fights Back*. Distributed by Feminist Book Mart, Inc., 41–17 150th St., Flushing N.Y. 11355, rev. ed., 1974.

Firestone, Shulamith. *The Dialectic of Sex: The Case For Feminist Revolution*, New York: Morrow, 1974.

Frazier, Nancy, and Sadker, Myra. *Sexism in School and Society,* New York: Harper & Row, 1973.

Freeman, Jo. "The Building of the Gilded Cage," in *Radical Feminism,* edited by Anne Koedt and Ellen Levine Rapone. New York: Quadrangle Books, 1973.

Fuller, Mary M. "In Business the Generic Pronoun 'he' is Non-job Related and Discriminatory," *Training and Development Journal,* May 1973, pp. 8–10.

Harrison, Barbara G. *Unlearning the Lie.* New York: Liveright, 1973. Morrow, 1974, paper.

Hartley, Ruth E. "Sex-Role Pressures and the Socialization of the Male Child," *Psychological Reports,* 1959, pp. 457–68.

Heatherington, E. M. "A Developmental Study of the Effects of Sex of the Dominant Parent on Sex-Role Preference, Identification, and Imitation of Children," *Journal of Personality and Social Psychology,* vol. 2, 1965, pp. 188–94.

Hirsch, L., ed. *The Block Book.* Washington, D.C.: National Association for the Education of Young Children, 1974. *Improving the Image of Women in Textbooks.* Glenview, Ill.: Scott Foresman, 1972.

Joffee, Carole. "Sex Role Socialization and the Nursery School: As the Twig Is Bent," *Journal of Marriage and the Family,* August 1971, pp. 467–75.

Johnson, H. *The Art of Blockbuilding.* New York: Bank Street Publication, 1933.

Johnson, Laurie Olsen, ed. *Nonsexist Curricular Materials for Elementary Schools.* The Clearinghouse on Women's Studies, Feminist Press, Box 334, Old Westbury, N.Y. 11568, 1974.

Lakoff, Robin. "You Are What You Say," *Ms. Magazine,* July 1974, 65–67.

Lee, Patrick, and Gropper, Nancy B. "Sex-Role Culture and Educational Practice," *Harvard Educational Review,* vol. 44, no. 3, August 1974, pp. 369–410.

Maccoby, Eleanor E., ed. *The Development of Sex-Role Differences.* Stanford, Calif.: Stanford University Press, 1966.

————, and Jacklin, Carol Nagy. *Psychology of Sex Differences.* Stanford, Calif.: Stanford University Press, 1975.

Mischel, W. "Sex Typing and Socialization" in P. H. Mussen, ed., *Carmichael's Manual of Child Psychology*, vol. 2. New York: John Wiley & Sons, 1970.

Mitchell, E. "The Learning of Sex Roles Through Toys and Books: A Women's View," *Young Children*, vol. 28, 1973, pp. 226–31.

Moberg, Verne. *A Child's Right to Equal Reading: Exercises in the Liberation of Children's Books from the Limitations of Sexual Stereotypes*. The Feminist Press, Box 334, Old Westbury, N.Y. 11568, 1972.

Mussen, Paul, and Distler, Luther. "Child Rearing Antecedents of Masculine Identification in Kindergarten Boys," *Child Development*, vol. 31, no. 1, 1960, pp. 89–100.

Pogrebin, Letty Cottin. "Down With Sexist Upbringing," *Ms. Magazine*, preview issue, Spring 1972.

Rudolph, M., and Cohen, D. *Kindergarten, A Year of Learning*. New York: Appleton-Century-Crofts, 1964.

Rothbart, M. K., and Maccoby, E. E. "Parents Differential Reactions to Sons and Daughters," *Journal of Personal & Social Psychology*, vol. 4, 1966, pp. 237–43.

Saario, T. M., Tittle, C. K., and Jacklin, J. N. "Sex-Role Stereotyping," *Harvard Educational Review*, vol. 43, no. 3, August 1973, pp. 386–416.

Stark, E. *Blockbuilding*. Washington, D.C.: National Education Association, 1960.

Weitzman, Lenore, and others. "Sex-role Socialization in Picture Books for Pre-school Children," *American Journal of Sociology*, vol. 77, no. 6, May 1972, pp. 1125–50.

Women on Words and Images. *Dick and Jane as Victims*, P.O. Box 2163, Princeton, N.J., 1972.

———. *Channeling Children: Sex Stereotyping on Prime Time TV*. 1975.

CHECKLIST FOR A NON-SEXIST CLASSROOM *

The following checklist is meant to be used as a self-evaluating tool. For the best results, you should be honest

---

* This questionnaire was prepared by Felicia George, Assistant Project Director, Women's Action Alliance.

112

in answering all questions. Answers should reflect the way you feel, act, or think NOW and not how you would like to think or act nor how you think you should feel.

Classroom

1. Are there the same number of pictures of girls as pictures of boys displayed around the room?_____ If not, how many are pictures of girls?_____ pictures of boys?_____

   Do the pictures of girls show girls involved in active play?_____

   Do the pictures of boys show boys in contemplative or caring roles?_____

   Do the pictures of girls show girls displaying "positive" behaviors, such as: making decisions_____ leading_____ helping_____ solving problems_____ and "negative" behaviors, such as: crying (or sad)_____ hitting_____ getting into trouble_____

   Are there more pictures of one type than the other?_____ If yes, which type?_____

   Do the pictures of boys show boys displaying "positive" behaviors, such as: helping_____ leading_____ making decisions_____ solving problems_____ and "negative" behaviors, such as: crying (or sad)_____ hitting_____ getting into trouble_____

   Are there more pictures of one type than the other?_____ If yes, which type?_____

   The majority of pictures of boys are_____.

   The majority of pictures of girls are_____.
2. In which areas of the room do you display pictures of both sexes involved in that area's activity?
   blocks_____ dramatic play (doll corner)_____ art_____ woodworking_____ manipulative_____ reading_____ science_____ other (specify)_____

   Are all areas attractive, i.e. organized, clearly labeled, decorated with pictures of interesting items?

dramatic play Y N   blocks Y N   science Y N   music
Y N   woodworking Y N   cooking Y N   manipulative
Y N   reading Y N

Are pictures of male and female adults engaged in comparable activities displayed? Y N
which activity(ies)_____ which sex(es)_____

Keep a record for one week (chosen randomly) of activities participated in by each sex: (sample record form)

	MON:	TUES:	WED:	THURS:	FRI:	TOTAL
Girls						
Boys						

Attitude:

1. Do girls and boys play in all areas of the classroom?
   Y N   If not, in which areas don't girls play?_____
   in which areas don't boys play?_____

Keep a record of the areas each child plays in. (Mark child's initial in box for area each time he/she plays in that area for one week).

		GIRLS	BOYS
A.	Doll Corner		
	Art		
	Cooking		
B.	Blocks		
	Woodwork		
C.	Sand/Water		
	Reading		

Are there girls who play only in area A? Y N   If yes, how would you characterize these girls?_____

Are there girls who play only in areas A and C? Y N   If yes, how would you characterize these girls?_____

Are there girls who play only in areas B and C? Y N   If yes, how would you characterize these girls?_____

Are there boys who play only in area B? Y N   If yes, how would you characterize these boys?_____

Are there boys who play only in areas B and C? Y N   If yes, how would you characterize these boys?_____

Are there boys who play only in areas A and C? Y N   If yes, how would you characterize these boys?_____

Are there boys and girls who play in areas A, B, and C? Y N   If yes, how would you characterize these children?_____

2. From the following list check those activities that you do not present to your class?
woodworking_____ active games_____ sewing_____
cooking_____ music_____ reading_____ electricity
_____ dance_____

Why don't you?_____
_____

Do you plan a greater % of noisy or quiet activities? noisy_____ quiet_____

Do you plan a greater % of messy or neat activities? messy_____ neat_____

Do you disapprove of noisy girls? Y N   noisy boys? Y N
noisy girls more than noisy boys? Y N   noisy boys more than noisy girls Y N

3. Check the statements which best describe your reaction to the children's appearance.

Girls
"What a pretty dress!"
"That's a good warm sweater to wear on a cold day."
"You came in like a big girl today."
"Linda is wearing ribbons!"
"Those are good shoes for running."
"You look nice today."
"Short sleeves are comfortable on a warm day like today."

Boys
"What a handsome suit!"
"That's a good warm sweater to wear on a cold day."
"You came in like a big boy today."
"Mark has a part in his hair!"
"Those are good shoes for running."
"You look nice today."
"Short sleeves are comfortable on a warm day like today."

4. List the following attributes under the column that you feel they most accurately describe.

confident	happy	intelligent	passive	ambitious
tender	vain	independent	protective	emotional
strong	brave	responsible	weak	attractive
tough	timid	competent	aggressive	considerate
active	stoic	forceful	talkative	fearful
	objective	dependent	creative	

Boys	*Girls*